S0-FCR-960

THE RELIGIONS OF DEMOCRACY

JUDAISM, CATHOLICISM, PROTESTANTISM
IN CREED AND LIFE

By

LOUIS FINKELSTEIN
J. ELLIOT ROSS
WILLIAM ADAMS BROWN

THE DEVIN-ADAIR COMPANY
NEW YORK
1946

FOURTH PRINTING

PRINTED IN THE UNITED STATES OF AMERICA

CONTENTS

☆

INTRODUCTION

IN ENTITLING this book The Religions of Democracy we have in mind the belief in the worth and rights of the individual which characterizes all three of the faiths with which it deals. Based upon religion, it repudiates all forms of tyranny. This affirmation of the supreme importance of the individual lies at the foundation of all true democracy.

This volume presents in outline the three faiths to one or the other of which the citizens of the United States, for the most part, adhere. It does not engage in controversy, and the writers make no effort to justify the beliefs and practices which they report. Nor is there any purpose to make converts from one faith to another, but merely to state and interpret the faith of each group to other groups in the interest of understanding.

If Jews, Catholics and Protestants are to live happily and cooperatively together it is imperative that they should understand one another. Such understanding will disclose, on the one hand, the limitations and, on the other, the possibilities of cooperation. As Americans all, they have the same obligations as citizens of the one country and must work cordially together for the common welfare within the communities which are their common homes. Each must stand for the rights of all. Together they must resist the prejudices that would divide them and set them in hostile camps.

The most fruitful source of prejudice is ignorance. We are likely to fear that which we do not fully comprehend. Suspicion is often the product of misunderstanding. When we are rightly informed as to the beliefs and practices of our neighbors, we may still disagree with them profoundly but we are not as likely to dislike, distrust or malign them.

Without minimizing the importance of the conscientious convictions wherein each differs from the others, we need constantly to bear in mind that Jews, Catholics and Protestants possess a valuable fund of common faith and a wide realm of common ideal and purpose.

Here in the United States those of all three faiths have an equal stake in the perpetuation of our free institutions and each group, in its own way, has made its own contribution to their establishment and maintenance. All are agreed that, to be permanent, democracy requires the support of religious sanctions.

Protestants, Catholics and Jews alike affirm their allegiance to the American doctrine of religious freedom. They are in general accord, also, as to what that doctrine involves.

Anyone who has thought about what religious freedom implies, knows that it is not a simple question. Is it a violation of religious freedom, for example, to forbid the practice of "suttee"—the burning of a widow on the funeral pyre of her dead husband—or polygamy? No, for religious freedom is not license, and individuals or groups of individuals should not be permitted, under the plea of following their consciences, to do what is offensive to the consciences of a great many others. Doukobars, for example, may be perfectly conscientious in their characteristic processions, but the civil authority is certainly not violating any sound principle of religious freedom in preventing such processions because they offend the consciences of others.

The American principle of religious liberty, expressed very tersely, is simply this: that the State should not forbid its citizens to do what their religion requires, nor require them to do what their religion forbids. The principle assumes, of course, that what a citizen's religion forbids or requires does not involve the violation of the fundamental human rights of those who hold different convictions from his own.

If the State commanded the faithful adherent of any religion to do what his conscience teaches him is sinful, Catholics, Jews and Protestants would agree in considering it to be a violation of religious freedom. This would be the case whatever might be the basis on which conscientious conviction is shaped. The fact, for instance, that in many things the Catholic conscience is formed by an ecclesiastical authority and that of some other groups by a more democratic process, is irrelevant. The American doctrine of the freedom of religion respects the religious conscience whatever may be the source of its convictions, always provided that such convictions do not infringe upon the rights of others.

For the State to *allow* citizens to do what is against the religious tenets and the conscience of some of them, as, for example, to divorce one lawful spouse and marry another, is not to use the power of the State to force any citizen to violate his conscience. Men would still be free to follow conscience. On the other hand, if the State, after some war in which so many men were killed that there were twice as many women as men, commanded every man to have two wives, this would be a clear violation of conscience.

A corollary of the principle of religious freedom is that of the separation of Church and State. Jews, Catholics and Protestants in America alike heartily support that doctrine as defined in the Constitution. It means that the Church and the State is each supreme in its own field and that neither should encroach upon the realm that properly belongs to the other.

The American doctrine of the separation of Church and State implies that men are free to believe as their consciences require and that they owe to the State obedience only in civil matters.

The charter of Rhode Island, which remained in force for one hundred and eighty years, represents Charles II as saying:

> Our royal will and pleasure is that no person within said colony any time hereafter shall be any wise molested, punished, disquieted, or called in question, for any differences in opinion in matters of religion, that do not actually disturb the civil peace of our said colony: but that all and every person and persons may, from time to time, and at all times hereafter, freely and fully have and enjoy his and their own judgments and consciences, in matters of religious concernments, throughout the tract of land hereafter mentioned.

The doctrine so defined was generally adopted in the newly formed United States and received the support not only of Protestants, but of Catholic and Jewish leaders. It is affirmed in the organic law of the land in the First Amendment to the Constitution which declares: "Congress shall make no law respecting an establishment of religion, or prohibiting the free exercise thereof." This does not mean that Congress abjures all interest in religion, nor does it propose to divorce religion from society.

It does mean that there shall be no state church in the United States in the sense in which such establishments exist in other lands and that no ecclesiastical organization shall enjoy rights or privileges that are not equally extended to all. It does mean that men shall be free to worship as they choose.

The American system, though not anti-religious or what Europeans call "laic," makes no distinction between religions. All citizens, no matter to what church they belong, or whether they belong to none, enjoy the same civil rights and immunities. Whatever claims to the exclusive possession of truth any religious group or church may make, it may also believe that as God tolerates the affiliation of creatures with many different religions, so the State in America should tolerate this condition.

The authors who have written the sections of this book whose names they respectively bear are competent in the fields with which they deal. Dr. Louis Finkelstein is President of the Jewish Theological Seminary of America, where he has taught for twenty years. Author of many books, his scholarship is recognized far beyond Jewish circles. Father John Elliot Ross holds the degree of Ph.D. from the Catholic University, and of D.D. from a Papal University in Rome. He has had a distinguished career as teacher of theology and religious education, and as chaplain to Catholic students in important educational institutions. He has found time to write more than a dozen books. Professor William Adams Brown is widely honored in this country and abroad for his leadership in the ecumenical movement, including the Universal Christian Council for Life and Work, the World Conference on Faith and Order, and the World Council of Churches. He is emeritus professor in applied theology in Union

Theological Seminary where he taught for forty-four years. In a score of books he has interpreted the Christian faith for modern readers.

To Dr. Brown's treatment of Protestantism we have appended *The Affirmation of Unity* adopted by the World Conference on Faith and Order, held in Edinburgh in 1937. That this document was adopted by representatives of the major Protestant denominations throughout the world and by representatives of the Eastern Orthodox Churches meeting together is significant of its very wide acceptance across church boundaries and of the growth of understanding and cooperation among communions that have been widely separated.

The writing of this book has been a cooperative venture, in which the participants have been in constant consultation with one another and each author has submitted his manuscript for the scrutiny and comment of the other two.

It is to promote the degree of intelligent understanding upon which all amity and mutual appreciation must depend that this book has been written. Here in this free land Jews, Catholics and Protestants are bound up together in one bundle of life and share a common fortune. It is imperative that they should understand each other and also that they should stand together for the things that they alike cherish.

Standing aloof and apart, and mistrusting one another Jews, Catholics and Protestants in Europe have been made victims of pagan, totalitarian forces. In America the only safe course is for them to dwell together in mutual respect and appreciation and to cooperate in the maintenance of each other's and their common rights.

The spirit of this book is thoroughly in accord with

that of the National Conference of Christians and Jews under whose auspices it is issued. Without debate or argument and with the single purpose of making clear the faith by which men live and the kind of conduct that such faith requires, its authors offer their contributions to the cause of concord and understanding.

ROBERT A. ASHWORTH,
Editorial Secretary,
The National Conference of Christians and Jews

PART I

THE BELIEFS AND PRACTICES OF JUDAISM

BY LOUIS FINKELSTEIN

☆

BIBLIOGRAPHY

Judaism, I. Epstein, London, 1939.

The Jewish Religion, Michael Friedlaender, New York, 1923.

Laws and Customs, Gerald Friedlander, London, 1921.

The Jewish Religion, Julius Greenstone, Philadelphia, 1920.

Judaism as Creed and Life, Morris Joseph, London, 1903.

The Meaning of Modern Jewish Religion, M. M. Kaplan, New York, 1937.

Reform Movement in Judaism, David Philipson, New York, 1931.

I. INTRODUCTION

JUDAISM is a way of life which endeavors to transform virtually every human action into a means of communion with God. Through this communion with God, the Jew is enabled to make his contribution to the establishment of the Kingdom of God and the brotherhood of men on earth. So far as its adherents are concerned, Judaism seeks to extend the concept of right and wrong to every aspect of their behavior. Jewish rules of conduct apply not merely to worship, ceremonial, and justice between man and man, but also to such matters as philanthropy, personal friendships and kindnesses, intellectual pursuits, artistic creation, courtesy, the preservation of health, and the care of diet.[1]

So rigorous is this discipline, as ideally conceived in Jewish writings, that it may be compared to those specified for members of religious orders in other faiths. A casual conversation or a thoughtless remark may, for instance, be considered a grave violation of Jewish Law. It is forbidden, not merely as a matter of good form, but of religious law, to use obscene language, to rouse a person to anger, or to display unusual ability in the presence of the handicapped. The ceremonial observances are equally detailed. The ceremonial Law expects that each Jew will pray

[1] Without desiring to ascribe to them any responsibility for this paper, I record with deep gratitude the assistance in its preparation given by colleagues from different schools of Jewish thought. These include Rabbis Max Arzt, Ben Zion Bokser, Samuel S. Cohon, Judah Goldin, Israel M. Goldman, Simon Greenberg, David de Sola Pool, Samuel Schulman, and Aaron J. Tofield.

thrice every day, if possible at the synagogue; to recite a blessing before and after each meal; to thank God for any special pleasure, such as a curious sight, the perfume of a flower, or the receipt of good news, wear a fringed garment about his body; to recite certain passages from Scripture each day; and to don *tephillin* (cubical receptacles containing certain Biblical passages) during the morning prayers.

The decisions regarding right and wrong under given conditions are not left for the moment, but are formulated with great care in the vast literature created by the Jewish religious teachers. At the heart of this literature are the Hebrew Scriptures, usually described as the Old Testament, consisting of the Five Books of Moses (usually called the *Torah*), the Prophets, and the Hagiographa. These works, particularly the Five Books of Moses, contain the prescriptions for human conduct composed under Divine inspiration. The ultimate purpose of Jewish religious study is the application of the principles enunciated in the Scriptures, to cases and circumstances which the principles do not explicitly cover.

Because Judaism is a way of life, no confession of faith can by itself make one a Jew. Belief in the dogmas of Judaism must be expressed in the acceptance of its discipline, rather than in the repetition of a verbal formula. But no failure either to accept the beliefs of Judaism or to follow its prescriptions is sufficient to exclude from the fold a member of the Jewish faith. According to Jewish tradition, the covenant between God and Moses on Mount Sinai included all those who were present and also all of their descendants. This covenant was reaffirmed in the days of Ezra and Nehemiah, when the people together with their leaders made "a sure covenant to walk in God's law, which was given to Moses the servant of God, and to observe and do all the commandments of the Lord our Lord, and His ordinances and His statutes" (Nehemiah 10.30). To apply the words used by Scripture in another connection, this covenant has thus been made binding upon the Jews, "and upon their seed, and upon all such as joined themselves unto them" (Esther 9.27). There is therefore no need for any ceremony to admit a Jewish child into the faith of Judaism. Born in a Jewish household, he becomes at once "a child of the covenant." The fact that the child has Jewish parents involves the assumption of the obligations which God has placed on these parents and their descendants.

This concept of the inheritance of religious traditions does not imply any sense of racial differentiation. The concept derives simply from the belief that a person may assume binding obligations not only for himself, but also for his descendants. Thus anyone who is converted to Judaism assumes the obligation to observe its discipline, and makes this obligation binding on his descendants forever, precisely as if he had been an Israelite, standing with Moses, before Mount Sinai on the day of the Revelation.

The ancestry of the proselyte and therefore his "race," are quite irrelevant matters. Whether he be of Arabic background, like Queen Helene, or Roman, like Aquila, or Chazar, like the members of the south Russian kingdom which became converted to Judaism in the eighth century of the Christian era, or Norman like Obadiah, the well known Crusader who became a proselyte, or Polish, like the famous Count Valentine Potocki of the eighteenth century, his descendants, from the point of view of Judaism, would all be bound by his obligation to follow the laws and customs of Judaism.

On the other hand, in view of the Jewish attitude to other monotheistic faiths, it is considered improper for a Jew to urge a member of another faith to become a Jew. Indeed, a person who desires to adopt Judaism must be told of all the difficulties which are inherent in affiliation with the faith. Only a person who persists in his desire to become a Jew, and demonstrates that his desire is based on no mundane motive, may be accepted into the Jewish fold.

Because of the special place which the home occupies in Judaism as a center of religious life and worship, almost coordinate with the synagogue itself, Judaism holds it essential that both parties to a Jewish marriage be members of the Jewish faith. There is, of course, no objection to marriage with a sincere convert to Judaism. But it is not possible for the home to function in the manner prescribed by Jewish law unless both husband and wife are of the Jewish faith.

In the case of a mixed marriage, the status of the children is determined by the faith of the mother, as the greatest influence in their lives. The children of a Christian mother are considered Christians; the children of a Jewish mother are considered Jews. The Jewish partner in such a mixed marriage is considered living in continual transgression of Jewish law, but remains, like those who deviate from the Law in other respects, within the fold of Judaism, entirely subject to the duties and obligations placed on other Jews.

While no one outside of the Jewish faith is bound by the rules of Jewish ceremonial discipline, Judaism draws a distinction between the adherents of monotheistic faiths, including Christianity and Islam, which are recognized as making a distinctive contribution to the realization of the Kingdom of God on earth, and non-monotheistic faiths. The various regulations which Judaism, like early Christianity, established to prevent reversion to paganism, obviously have no application to the relationship between Jews and their neighbors in Christian and Mohammedan countries. A Jew may not enter a building dedicated to idol-worship even to protect himself from inclement weather; and of course, he cannot participate in any festivity dedicated to any form of idol-worship.

These ceremonial rules are intended to register a protest against paganism; they do not place the pagan in any inferior position with regard to Jewish law or ethic. According to Philo and Josephus, it is a violation of Jewish law for a Jew to speak with disrespect of the gods of any people, for the verse, "Thou shalt not revile God" (Exodus 22.27), is interpreted as applying to all gods. While this interpretation is not accepted in the rabbinic tradition, it does express the spirit with which Judaism approaches all systems of belief, regardless of the extent of their difference from itself.

This spirit is expressed in the principle that every rule of moral conduct which a Jew must observe toward another Jew applies also to relations with persons of other faiths. The laws of justice, kindness, and charity, as well as the obligation to visit the sick, bury the dead, support the needy, must be assumed for all people.

Like other religions, Judaism can be, and indeed has been practiced under various forms of civil government: monarchical, semi-monarchical, feudal, democratic, and totalitarian. The members of the Jewish faith, like those of other religions, regard themselves as citizens or subjects of their respective states. In all synagogues prayers are offered for the safety of the government of the country;

and in the ancient Temple of Jerusalem daily sacrifices were offered on behalf of the Imperial Roman Government, as long as Palestine remained under its dominion. This patriotic loyalty to the state has often persisted in the face of cruel persecution. The principle followed has been that formulated by the ancient teacher, Rabbi Haninah, "Pray for the welfare of the government; for without fear of the government, men would have swallowed each other up alive."

Despite this ability to adjust itself to the exigencies of any form of temporal government, Judaism, like other faiths derived from the Prophets, has always upheld the principles of the Fatherhood of God and the dignity and worth of Man as the child and creature of God; and its ideals are more consistent with those of democracy than any other system of government.

The most vigorous and consistent effort to formulate the discipline of Judaism in terms of daily life was that made in ancient Palestine and Babylonia. The Palestinian schools devoted to this purpose were founded in the second century before the Christian era, and flourished in their original form for six centuries and in a somewhat altered form until the Crusades. The Babylonian schools were founded in the third century of the Christian era, and ended the first and most significant phase of their activity about three hundred years later.

The rules of conduct worked out in the discussions of these academies form the substance of Jewish Law. In arriving at these precepts, the ancient teachers were guided by their desire to know the will of God. So far as possible they sought to discover His will through an intensive study of the Scriptures. Where Scripture offered no clear guidance they tried to ascertain His will by applying its general principle or moral right. In addition, they had a number of oral traditions, going back to antiquity, which they regarded as supplementary to the written Law, and equal to it in authority and inspiration.

The high purpose of the discussions made them of monumental importance to Judaism. As a result, they were committed to memory by eager and faithful disciples, until the memorized material grew to such proportions that it had to be reduced to writing. The work in which the discussions were thus preserved is known as the Talmud. As there were two groups of academies, differing slightly from one another in their interpretation of the Law, and widely in their manner of approach to the subject, we have two Talmudim, that of Palestine and that of Babylonia. Both are considered authoritative guides for Jewish Law. Where they disagree, the Babylonian Talmud is, for historical reasons, considered the more authoritative.

II. THE PLACE OF STUDY IN JUDAISM

It is quite impossible to understand Judaism without an appreciation of the place which it assigns to the study and practice of the Talmudic Law. Doing the will of God is the primary spiritual concern of the Jew. Therefore, to this day, he must devote considerable time not merely to the mastery of the content of the Talmud, but also to training in its method of reasoning. The study of the Bible and the Talmud is thus far more than a pleasing intellectual exercise, and is itself a means of communion with God. According to some teachers, this study is the highest form of such communion imaginable.[2]

Because the preservation of the Divine will regarding human conduct is basic to all civilization, none of the commandments is more important than that of studying and teaching the Law. The most sacred object in Judaism is the scroll containing the Five Books of Moses. Every synagogue must contain at least one copy of it. The scroll must be placed in a separate Ark, before which burns the eternal light. The position of this Ark in the synagogue is in the direction of Jerusalem; everyone turns toward the Ark in prayer. When the scroll is taken from the Ark for the purpose of reading, all those present must rise. No irreverent or profane action may be performed in a room which contains a scroll, nor may a scroll be moved from place to place except for the performance of religious rites. From

[2] See the essay on "Study as a Mode of Worship," by Professor Nathan Isaacs, in *The Jewish Library*, edited by Rabbi Leo Jung, 1928, pp. 51-70.

time to time the scroll must be examined to ascertain that its writing is intact.

The preparation of the scroll is a task requiring much care, erudition, and labor. It is usually done by a professional copyist called a *sofer* (scribe). The text is written on sheets of parchment, especially prepared for the purpose. Only skins of animals permitted for food, in accordance with Leviticus 11.1-9 and Deuteronomy 14.3-9, are used. The whole work is then attached at the beginning and at the end to wooden rods, so that it can be rolled in the form of a scroll.

The ink used in writing must be black, and should be indelible. Before beginning to copy the text, the scribe must say, "I am about to write this book as a sacred scroll of the Law." He repeats a similar formula every time he is about to copy the Divine Name, saying, "I am writing this word as the sacred Name."

Like other Semitic languages, Hebrew requires only a consonantal text for reading: the vowels are omitted in classical texts. Hence the scroll of the Five Books of Moses contains only the consonantal text. This text is fixed by tradition, almost to the last detail. Even such matters as division into paragraphs and sections, and the special size of certain letters, which are particularly large or particularly small, is determined. The texts of all the extant scrolls are thus virtually identical. Any significant deviation from the traditional text makes a scroll unfit for use, and must be corrected as soon as it is discovered. No decorations or illuminations are permitted in the scrolls intended for the public service. Tradition prescribes, however, that certain poetic portions are to be written in verse form, and that certain letters shall have little coronets adorning them.

No less important than this homage paid to the scroll as symbol of the Law, is that paid to the living Law itself. Fully three-fourths of the Hebrew literature produced within the first nineteen centuries of the Christian era, is devoted to the elucidation of the Law. The best minds in Judaism have been devoted to its study. Every parent is required to teach his child its basic elements. Its study is considered vital not only for the guidance it offers in the practice of Judaism, but for liberation from the burden of secular ambition and anxieties. The study of the Law is believed to be a foretaste of the immortal life, for the sages of the Talmud believed that Paradise itself could offer men no nearer communion with God than the opportunity of discovering His will in the study of the Law.

The Talmud derives its authority from the position held by the ancient academies. The teachers of these academies, both those of Babylonia and of Palestine, were considered the rightful successors of the older *Sanhedrin* or Supreme Court, which before the destruction of Jerusalem (in the year 70 of the Christian era) was the arbiter of Jewish Law and custom. The Sanhedrin derived its authority from the statement in Deuteronomy 17.8-13, that whenever a question of interpretation of the Law arises, it is to be finally decided by the sages and priests in Jerusalem.

At the present time, the Jewish people have no living central authority comparable in status to the ancient Sanhedrin or the later academies. Therefore any decision regarding Jewish religion must be based on the Talmud, as the final résumé of the teachings of those authorities when they existed. The right of an individual to decide questions of religious Law depends entirely on his knowledge of the Bible, the Talmud, and the later manuals based on them, and upon his fidelity to their teachings. Those who have acquired this knowledge are called rabbis. There is no sharp distinction in religious status between the rabbi and the layman in Judaism. The rabbi is simply a layman especially learned in Scripture and Talmud. Nor is there any hierarchical organization or government among the rabbis of the world. Yet some rabbis, by virtue of their especial distinction in learning, by common consent come to be regarded as superior authorities on questions of Jewish Law. Difficult and complicated issues are referred to them for clarification.

To be recognized as a rabbi, a Talmudic student customarily is ordained. Traditionally, the authority to act as rabbi may be conferred by any other rabbi. It is usual, however, for students at various theological schools to receive this authority from their teachers. In America, there are several rabbinical schools, each of which ordains its graduates in the manner in which degrees are conferred on graduates of other institutions of learning. At present (1941) the best known of these schools are as follows:

Hebrew Theological College, Chicago
Hebrew Union College, Cincinnati
Jewish Institute of Religion, New York City
Jewish Theological Seminary of America, New York City
Rabbi Isaac Elchanan Theological Seminary, New York City

There is considerable variation among the interpretations of Judaism taught at these seminaries, and consequently there is a considerabie difference in emphasis on the subjects included in their respective curricula. This has resulted from the fact that during the past century various groups of rabbis, primarily in Germany and America, have claimed authority not merely to interpret, but also to amend Talmudic, and even Biblical Law. These rabbis are known as reform rabbis, and their congregations as reform congregations. Of the rabbis who adhere to traditional Judaism, some reject any significant innovations from customary practice; these rabbis are called orthodox. Others maintain that Jewish law is a living tradition, subject to change, but they insist that such changes must be made in accordance with traditional canons for the interpretation and development of rabbinic law. These rabbis are usually called "conservative."

The differences between the various groups of American rabbis have not led to any sectarian schism. Although the difference in practice between the traditional and reform groups is considerable, each accepts the other as being within the fold of Judaism. It is possible for them to do so, because of the principle that even an unobservant or a heretical Jew does not cease to be a member of the covenant made between God and Israel at the time of the Revelation. Only actual rejection of Judaism, by affiliation with another faith, is recognized as separating one from the Jewish community.[3] So long as a member of the Jewish faith has not by overt act or word and of his own free will declared himself a member of another religion, other Jews are bound to regard him as one of their own faith, and to seek his return to its practice and beliefs.

[3] The extent to which even conversion to another faith affects the status of an individual within Judaism, is a subject of considerable discussion in rabbinical literature. Many authorities consider such a person a Jew, despite his conversion. The prevailing opinion, however, recognizes as effective the voluntary separation of a person from Judaism.

III. THE PLACE OF ETHICS IN JUDAISM

The ceremonial discipline is considered obligatory only on members of the Jewish faith, but the ethical element in Judaism is universal in scope. The commandment against murder is explicitly stated in Scripture to have been revealed to Noah (Genesis 9.5); and therefore applies to all humankind. By analogy, the commandments against theft, cruelty to animals, sexual license, blasphemy, idol-worship, and the violation of civil justice, are considered to be universal. Those who observe these fundamental laws are considered "the righteous of the peoples of the world," who will partake in the resurrection and in immortality.

One further distinction is made between the ethical and ceremonial content of Judaism. When faced with the danger of death, one may violate any of the commandments, save only those against murder, sexual license, and idolatry. This rule does not apply in the event of a religious persecution. When a government undertakes to suppress the observance of Judaism, it becomes the duty of the Jew to submit to martyrdom rather than deviate from his faith, in even a slight matter.

The duty of accepting martyrdom, either for the ethical Law in the normal course of events, or for the whole of the Law in times of persecution, is called *Kiddush ha-Shem,* (sanctification of the Name of God). Any violation of this duty is called the profanation of the Name of God, *Hillul ha-Shem.* These terms may also be applied to situations which do not call for martyrdom, but where it is possible to increase or lessen respect for religious faith through action. Anyone who through sacrifice and saintliness brings others to more profound recognition of God, "sanctifies" the Name of God. But anyone whose actions bring religion generally and Judaism in particular into disrespect, is guilty of *Hillul ha-Shem.* Because of this principle, religious leaders are expected to be particularly careful of their ethical conduct, for even the slightest deviation from propriety on their part naturally casts aspersion on the whole faith. Similarly, any impropriety on the part of a Jew in his relations with members of other faiths tends to decrease respect for Judaism as a faith, and is therefore "a profanation of the Name of God."

The application of the ethical teachings of Judaism to every aspect of daily life has necessarily involved the creation and development of a system of civil law. Like contemporary Christians, the Jews of the Talmudic period believed it wrong to resort to the pagan courts of their time for adjudication of civil differences. Not only did the Jewish conception of justice frequently differ from that of the pagans, but the pagan courts were often corrupt, and almost always cruel. The tradition opposing the use of civil courts for adjudication of civil disputes, persisted during the Middle Ages. For many centuries secular courts were few and inaccessible, and even in later periods their judgments were generally considered unfair. Only with the enlightenment of the eighteenth and nineteenth centuries, and the disappearance of the ghettos, have Jews become accustomed to apply to secular courts of justice for settlement of their litigation. However, it is a fundamental principle of Talmudic Law that the civil law of a country is binding, and a Jewish court would necessarily have to take cognizance of the civil law on any disputed point.

The necessity of dealing with civil litigation compelled the Talmudic sages and their mediaeval successors to give much attention to this aspect of the Jewish law. Hence, about one-fourth of the Babylonian Talmud, and a proportionate share of later rabbinic literature, is devoted to questions of civil law. The latest compilation of this law is to be found in the *Hoshen Mishpat,* the fourth volume of Rabbi Joseph Caro's famous code, the *Shulhan Aruk.*

The Jewish civil law is frequently applied even today in the adjudication of disputes arising among religious functionaries, and is sometimes used as a basis for arbitration agreements.

But the Jewish conception of justice transcends the realm of civil law. Justice includes all ethical conduct, as well as philanthropy. Indeed, the word for charity in rabbinic Hebrew is *sedakah,* or righteousness. Under certain circumstances, Talmudic law actually permits courts to compel a man to do his duty by the community or by individuals, beyond the letter of the law.

As a rule, a Jew is expected to give between one-tenth and one-fifth of his income to charitable purposes. To give less than one-tenth is to fail in duty to the community; to give more than a fifth may involve injustice to the immediate family. Beyond provision of material assistance for the needy and suffering, lies the duty of encouraging them with personal attention and kind words, of recognizing them as personal friends, and above all enabling them to help themselves. In his Code, Maimonides recognizes eight types of philanthropy, arranged according to their merit, as follows: 1) helping the needy to be self dependent by providing opportunity for work; 2) giving charity to the poor in such a way that neither the donor nor the recipient know one another; 3) giving charity in such a way that the donor can identify the recipient but the recipient cannot identify the donor; 4) giving in such a way that the recipient can identify the donor but the donor cannot identify the recipient; 5) giving in such a way that the donor and recipient know each other, provided the gift is made before it is requested; 6) giving after a request is made, provided the amount is sufficient to meet the need; 7) giving less than is needed, but with a kindly countenance; 8) giving less than is needed, and without a kindly countenance.

Judaism lays great stress on the importance of personal ethical relations between friends. The last of the Ten Commandments is a prohibition against "coveting" the blessings of a neighbor. Other regulations warn against talebearing, gossip, envy, and dislike of a neighbor. Any form of vengeance is also prohibited. If a person says to another, "Lend me your hatchet," and the second reply, "I will not lend you my hatchet today, because yesterday you refused to lend me your sickle," the second transgresses the commandment, "Thou shalt not take vengeance" (Leviticus 19.18). If the second reply, "I will lend you my hatchet, despite the fact that yesterday you refused to lend me your sickle," he transgresses the second half of the verse, "nor bear any grudge." The importance of these commandments in Judaism is such that onc of the most distinguished Jewish scholars of the eleventh century, Bahya ibn Pakuda, devoted a whole book to their analysis, the *Book of the Duties of the Heart*. In our own generation, the famous Rabbi Israel Meir Kahan (better known by the title of his book, *Chofetz Chayyim,* first published anonymously) devoted his life to warning against the transgression of these laws of ethical conduct. During the nineteenth century, there developed under the influence of Rabbi Israel Salanter (d. 1883) a whole group of students who refrained from conversation over long periods, in order to discipline themselves against the sin of "evil speech."

In accordance with the precept of Leviticus 19.17, Judaism considers every member of the faith responsible for the moral conduct of those neighbors over whom he is able to exert helpful influence. To see injustice done without protesting against it, is to participate in the injustice. To provoke a man to anger, is to partake of the sin of unjust anger. To permit an opposing litigant to take a false oath, is to share in the transgression of perjury; just as to listen to blasphemy, gossip, or talebearing is to be a party to them. The concept is summarized in the teaching of Rabbi Jacob that "a person, on whose account God has to inflict punishment on another, will not be admitted into the presence of God" (*Shabbat* 149b). The underlying principle of this teaching is the doctrine that a victim of injustice falls short of the ideal of Judaism to the extent that he fails to obtain Divine forgiveness for the person who acted unjustly toward him.

The public confession of sins prescribed for the Day of Atonement (see below) reflects this consciousness that every member of the community is to some extent responsible for the sins of every other member. The confession lists not only the sins which the average man is liable to commit through oversight, but also such sins as theft, unchastity, rendering false judgment, which are obviously not committed with the vast majority.

IV. THE BASIC CONCEPTS OF JUDAISM

The central doctrine of Judaism is the belief in the One God, the Father of all mankind. The first Hebrew words which a Jewish child learns are the confession of faith contained in the verse, "Hear, O Israel, the Lord is our God, the Lord is One," and every believing Jew hopes that as he approaches his end in the fulness of time, he will be sufficiently conscious to repeat this same confession. This monotheistic belief is subject to no qualification or compromise.

Another doctrine, which has become universal in Judaism, is the belief in the incorporeality of God, i.e., the belief that God has no physical, visible form.

A third doctrine, equally important, is the timelessness and omnipresence of God. As one of the Talmudic sages states, "God is the place of the Universe; the Universe cannot be regarded as His place."

While these concepts seem to put God far beyond the reach of even the most speculative human thought and imagination, Judaism insists also on God's accessibility to every human being who seeks Him. Every person may pray to Him, and His providence surrounds every phenomenon of human life. One of the great Palestinian sages of the third century of the Christian era, expressed this paradox in the following words: "Wherever Scripture describes the greatness of God, it also insists on His humility."

It is an error, however, according to Jewish theology to attribute to God even those good qualities which are found in man. To speak of God as being merciful in the sense in which man is merciful, is almost blasphemy, for in human life, mercy must sometimes be a mitigation of justice, and require a departure from courses dictated by wisdom and prudence. Such a deviation from justice or wisdom is necessitated by man's limited knowledge and vision, and the consequent necessity of distrusting his reason. In infinite wisdom and knowledge, justice and mercy necessarily become identical. When we speak of God as merciful, or kind, or loving, we do so in order to give expression to our human conceptions of Him. The manner of speech resembles in a way our necessarily partial and inadequate descriptions of physical phenomena. Yet just as descriptions of the physical universe, inadequate as they are, help us understand it, so our use of attributes enables us, to some extent at least, to appreciate God's ways with man.

It is a cardinal principle of Judaism that the highest form of piety is to perform the will of God out of love for Him, rather than out of fear of Him. To develop love for God, and to do His will, without any thought of the punishments He may inflict or the rewards He may offer, is one of the most difficult of disciplines. Many rabbini-sages endured personal affliction without murmur, but suffered anguish at the frustration of God's will in the world through human sin and waywardness.

While Judaism does not consider fear of punishment the principal reason for submission to Divine will, it recognizes the fact that disobedience necessarily entails suffering. This is not due to the fact that God, like an angry human parent or ruler, penalizes those who transgress His will. It is, rather, because the Divine discipline, as incorporated in Jewish tradition, is directed toward giving man as much happiness as can be obtained in life. Failure to conduct oneself in accordance with this discipline has the same effect on man's happiness, that failure to observe the rules of hygiene has on man's health. When we say that God punishes those who transgress His will, we mean that wicked actions inevitably deprive men of the happiness which would be in store for them if they followed the dictates of religion and ethics.

Because of God's love for men, He has made it possible for them to escape some of the consequences of error and sinful conduct. Most errors can be rectified through true repentance. Indeed, repentance sometimes makes it possible for the experience of error itself to become a virtue. The fact that a person has not lived in accordance with the discipline of religion does not, therefore, condemn him to suffering. It merely places on him the obligation to repent of his error, and return to God. He will find that in this return to God, he obtains the same measure of happiness awarded to those who have never committed a transgression.

However, repentance cannot always be achieved. If a man injures his neighbor, he will not be able to repent completely, or win peace of mind, until he has won the forgiveness of his neighbor. Rulers, who mislead their people, causing whole nations and races to indulge in wrong-doing, and to that extent deflecting the development of human civilization, cannot repent. They may be willing to rectify their wrong; but the power to rectify it will be beyond them. Finally, those who commit errors, thinking that they will be able to rectify them afterward, will find that they cannot really repent. The habit of hypocrisy in which they have indulged will vitiate any future efforts to rectify their errors.

To be effective, repentance must be more than sorrow or remorse; it must include a determination never again to commit the transgression, and a rearrangement of one's way of life so as to avoid the temptation to fall into the transgression. Thus if a person has been guilty of theft, repentance requires not merely restitution of the stolen article, and a determination never to steal again, but also a study of the motives which led to the theft, and an endeavor to prevent them from being effective in the future.

One of the most important stimulants to the good life is the companionship of well-chosen friends. It is a duty to select friends with a view to their probable influence on character. The person who deliberately chooses wicked companions, has only himself to blame if he finds himself falling into their manner of speech, and their daily habits.

The greatest possible deterrent from evil deeds or evil thoughts is the study of the Torah. By opening to man avenues of joy, creative endeavor, and happiness in the spiritual sphere, it removes from him the temptation to seek satisfaction of his human impulses to infringe on the rights of others or the commandments of God. If therefore a person finds himself facing temptation, he should turn more vigorously than ever to the study of the Torah.

Man differs from all other creatures, in that he is made "in the image of God." Because Judaism denies that God has any physical form, the image of God in this passage refers to man's mind. Created in the image of God, all persons must be accorded the respect due to this dignity which the Divine grace has accorded them. There can, therefore, be no differentiation between various human personalities in their status before God. From the time when the Prophet Amos declared, "Are ye not as the children of Ethiopians unto Me, O children of Israel" (9.7), until this day, Jewish religious teachers have continuously emphasized this doctrine. To Ben Azzai, the great teacher of the second century, the most inclusive principle of the whole Law is to be found in the verse, "In the day that God created man, in the likeness of God made He him, male and female created He them" (Genesis 5.1-2). He considered this verse uniquely important because it expresses unequivocally the equality and dignity of all human beings, irrespective of nationality, sex, color, creed, or genealogical origin.

Bearing in himself the image of God, man is also, according to Jewish doctrine, endowed with immortality. As conceived by most Jewish theologians, immortality implies the endless persistence of the human personality. This personality is believed to find its complete expression in ultimate reunion with God, and to lose all concern with the divisions, rivalries and antagonisms, characteristic of physical life.

The attainment of this endless communion with God is the highest reward which man can attain, and its loss is the greatest punishment he can suffer. The evil of wickedness consists, therefore, not merely in the harm which it does to a man in his mundane life, but in the fact that it deprives him of immortal existence. There are many rabbinic authorities who believe, as do members of other faiths, that certain sinful people may obtain immortal life, after having undergone temporary suffering after death. It is held in the Talmud that "the punishment of the wicked in Gehenna does not exceed twelve months." According to Maimonides, this punishment consists of the keen awareness by the soul of its failure to utilize its opportunities for the service of God, and is analogous to the shame sometimes felt by adults for unwise and unkind acts in their youth. But it is a fundamental principle in Judaism, formulated as an ethical norm by Antigonus of Socho, one of the founders of rabbinic Judaism, that men "should not be as servants, who serve their Master with the expectation of receiving reward, but rather as servants who serve their Master, without expectation of receiving reward." In other words, the belief in immortal life is accepted as a metaphysical and theological truth. However, it should not be considered a motive for proper conduct. Proper conduct should be based (as indicated hereafter) simply on love of God and the desire to see His will performed in the world.

The revelation of the Divine will, through the Law, the Prophets, and the Holy Writings, was a singular phenomenon in history. The people to whom this revelation was made was the people of Israel, of which only a remnant now survives, known as the Jewish people. The fact that the people of Israel received the Law and heard the Prophets does not, according to Jewish teaching, endow them with any special privileges. But it does place upon them special responsibilities. These responsibilities, to observe the Law, to study it, and to explain it, are expressed in the term, "The Chosen People." God did not choose Israel to be the recipient of any mundane goods or prerogatives. He chose Israel to be His suffering servant, to bear persecution with patience, and by precept and example, to bring His word to all peoples of the world.

As indicated in this discussion, there is a wide variety of interpretation among rabbinical scholars, both ancient and modern, with regard to the concepts of Judaism. In some instances, the differences of interpretation are so great that it is difficult to speak of the concept as being basically or universally Jewish or rabbinic. There are thus a number of concepts, each having its own limited authority and following.

This applies also to a degree to the fundamental beliefs which have been brought together in the best known Jewish creed, that of Maimonides. According to this creed, there are thirteen basic dogmas in Judaism. They are as follows:

1. The belief in God's existence.
2. The belief in His unity.
3. The belief in His incorporeality.
4. The belief in His timelessness.
5. The belief that He is approachable through prayer.
6. The belief in prophecy.
7. The belief in the superiority of Moses to all other prophets.
8. The belief in the revelation of the Law, and that the Law as contained in our Pentateuch is that revealed to Moses.
9. The belief in the immutability of the Law.
10. The belief in Divine providence.
11. The belief in Divine justice.
12. The belief in the coming of the Messiah.
13. The belief in the resurrection and human immortality.

This creed has been incorporated in the Jewish liturgy, in the famous hymn, *Yigdal.* Nevertheless, various distinguished authorities, including such teachers as Hasdai Crescas and Joseph Albo, rejected the classification of the doctrines, and even denied the basic character of some of the doctrines themselves. Because of this divergence of opinion among the most eminent authorities on the subject, traditional Judaism cannot be described as having a universally accepted creed or formulation of its dogmas.

This has led to the assertion that "Judaism has no dogmas." The assertion is true, only to the extent already indicated. On the other hand, as Rabbi Albo pointed out, the requirement that Jews observe the discipline of the Law implies the belief in God, in Revelation, and in Divine providence.

Orthodox and conservative Jews have in general followed the example of the ancient and mediaeval teachers in avoiding any effort to formulate a generally adopted Jewish creed, beyond the informal consensus of opinion found in traditional writings. As a result, there is still wide latitude of interpretation of Judaism both among orthodox and conservative Jews.

Reform Jews have tried to formulate a definite platform outlining the principles on which they agree, and which they believe basic to Judaism. The most recent platform is that adopted at a meeting of the Central Conference of American Rabbis (the organization of American reform rabbis) in 1937. In this platform no effort is made to indicate the way reform Judaism deviates from the orthodox or conservative interpretation of Judaism. And, indeed, the platform does not contain much to which orthodox and conservative groups can take exception. It is rather in its implications than by its direct statements, that it deviates from tradition.

Known as the Columbus Platform from the city in which the meeting was held, the statement reads as follows:

"In view of the changes that have taken place in the modern world and the consequent need of stating anew the teachings of Reform Judaism, the Central Conference of American Rabbis makes the following declaration of principles. It presents them not as a fixed creed but as a guide for the progressive elements of Jewry.

I. Judaism and Its Foundations.

1. NATURE OF JUDAISM. Judaism is the historical religious experience of the Jewish people. Though growing out of Jewish life, its message is universal, aiming at the union and perfection of mankind under the sovereignty of God. Reform Judaism recognizes the principle of progressive development in religion and consciously applies this principle to spiritual as well as to cultural and social life.

Judaism welcomes all truth, whether written in the pages of Scripture or deciphered from the records of nature. The new discoveries of science, while replacing the older scientific views underlying our sacred literature, do not conflict with the essential spirit of religion as manifested in the consecration of man's will, heart and mind to the service of God and of humanity.

2. GOD. The heart of Judaism and its chief contribution to religion is the doctrine of the One, living God, Who rules the world through law and love. In Him all existence has its creative source and mankind its ideal of conduct. Though transcending time and space, He is the in-dwelling Presence of the world. We worship Him as the Lord of the universe and as our merciful Father.

3. MAN. Judaism affirms that man is created in the Divine image. His spirit is immortal. He is an active co-worker with God. As a child of God, he is endowed with moral freedom and is charged with the responsibility of overcoming evil and striving after ideal ends.

4. TORAH. God reveals Himself not only in the majesty, beauty and orderliness of nature, but also in the vision and moral striving of the human spirit. Revelation is a continuous process, confined to no one group and to no one age. Yet the people of Israel, through its prophets and sages, achieved unique insight in the realm of religious truth. The Torah, both written and oral, enshrines Israel's ever-growing consciousness of God and of the moral law. It preserves the historical precedents, sanctions and norms of Jewish life, and seeks to mould it in the

patterns of goodness and of holiness. Being products of historical processes, certain of its laws have lost their binding force with the passing of the conditions that called them forth. But as a depository of permanent spiritual ideals, the Torah remains the dynamic source of the life of Israel. Each age has the obligation to adapt the teachings of the Torah to its basic needs in consonance with the genius of Judaism.

5. ISRAEL. Judaism is the soul of which Israel is the body. Living in all parts of the world, Israel has been held together by the ties of common history, and above all, by the heritage of faith. Though we recognize in the group loyalty of Jews who have become estranged from our religious tradition, a bond which still unites them with us, we maintain that it is by its religion and for its religion that the Jewish people has lived. The non-Jew who accepts our faith is welcomed as a full member of the Jewish community.

In all lands where our people live, they assume and seek to share loyally the full duties and responsibilities of citizenship and to create seats of Jewish knowledge and religion. In the rehabilitation of Palestine, the land hallowed by memories and hopes, we behold the promise of renewed life for many of our brethren. We affirm the obligation of all Jewry to aid in its upbuilding as a Jewish homeland by endeavoring to make it not only a haven of refuge for the oppressed but also a center of Jewish culture and spiritual life.

Throughout the ages it has been Israel's mission to witness to the Divine in the face of every form of paganism and materialism. We regard it as our historic task to cooperate with all men in the establishment of the kingdom of God, of universal brotherhood, justice, truth and peace on earth. This is our Messianic goal.

II. Ethics.

6. ETHICS AND RELIGION. In Judaism religion and morality blend into an indissoluble unity. Seeking God means to strive after holiness, righteousness and goodness. The love of God is incomplete without the love of one's fellowmen. Judaism emphasizes the kinship of the human race, the sanctity and worth of human life and personality and the right of the individual to freedom and to the pursuit of his chosen vocation. Justice to all, irrespective of race, sect or class is the inalienable right and the inescapable obligation of all. The state and organized government exist in order to further these ends.

7. SOCIAL JUSTICE. Judaism seeks the attainment of a just society by the application of its teachings to the economic order, to industry and commerce, and to national and international affairs. It aims at the elimination of man-made misery and suffering, of poverty and degradation, of tyranny and slavery, of social inequality and prejudice, of ill-will and strife. It advocates the promotion of harmonious relations between warring classes on the basis of equity and justice, and the creation of conditions under which human personality may flourish. It pleads for the safeguarding of childhood against exploitation. It champions the cause of all who work and of their right to an adequate standard of living, as prior to the rights of property. Judaism emphasizes the duty of charity, and strives for a social order which will protect men against the material disabilities of old age, sickness and unemployment.

8. PEACE. Judaism, from the days of the prophets, has proclaimed to mankind the ideal of universal peace. The spiritual and physical disarmament of all nations has been one of its essential teachings. It abhors all violence and relies upon moral education, love and sympathy to secure human progress. It regards justice as the foundation of the well-being of nations and the condition of enduring peace. It urges organized international action for disarmament, collective security and world peace.

III. Religious Practice.

9. THE RELIGIOUS LIFE. Jewish life is marked by consecration to these ideals of Judaism. It calls for faithful participation in the life of the Jewish community as it finds expression in home, synagogue and school and in all other agencies that enrich Jewish life and promote its welfare.

The Home has been and must continue to be a stronghold of Jewish life, hallowed by the spirit of love and reverence, by moral discipline and religious observance and worship.

The Synagogue is the oldest and most democratic institution in Jewish life. It is the prime communal agency by which Judaism is fostered and preserved. It links the Jews of each community and unites them with all Israel.

The perpetuation of Judaism as a living force depends upon religious knowledge and upon the Education of each new generation in our rich cultural and spiritual heritage.

Prayer is the voice of religion, the language of faith and aspiration. It directs man's heart and mind Godward, voices the needs and hopes of the community, and reaches out after goals which invest life with supreme value. To deepen the spiritual life of our people, we must cultivate the traditional habit of communion with God through prayer in both home and synagogue.

Judaism as a way of life requires in addition to its moral and spiritual demands, the preservation of the Sabbath, festivals and Holy Days, the retention and development of such customs, symbols and ceremonies as possess inspirational value, the cultivation of distinctive forms of religious art and music and the use of Hebrew, together with the vernacular, in our worship and instruction.

These timeless aims and ideals of our faith we present anew to a confused and troubled world. We call upon our fellow Jews to rededicate themselves to them, and, in harmony with all men, hopefully and courageously to continue Israel's eternal quest after God and His kingdom."

None of the basic doctrines of Judaism deals expressly with the teachings, principles, or leading personalities of the younger religions derived from it. As Judaism antedates the origin of both Christianity and Mohammedanism, its views regarding both faiths are simply negative: it has not accepted their teachings. This attitude does not, however, prevent Judaism from endeavoring to appraise the significance and value of other faiths as spiritual and moral phenomena. Rabbi Jacob Emden (1697-1776), one of the foremost teachers in the history of Judaism, summarized the general Jewish view regarding Christianity in the following words:

"It is, therefore, a customary observation with me that the man of Nazareth wrought a double kindness to the world: On the one hand he fully supported the Torah of Moses, as already shown, for not one of our sages spoke more fervently about the eternal duty to fulfil the Law. On the other hand he brought much good to the Gentiles (if only they do not overturn his noble intention for them, as certain stupid people, who did not grasp the ultimate purpose of the New Testament have done; in fact, just recently I saw a book from the press whose author did not know himself what he had written; because, had he known what he had written, then his silence would have been more becoming than his speaking, and he would not have wasted his money nor spoiled the paper and the ink uselessly; just as among us are to be found stupid scholars who know not between their right hand and their left in the written, nor in the oral law, but deceive the world with a tongue that speaks arrogantly; but there are highly educated men of intelligence among the Christians, even as there are among the students of our Torah a few outstanding individuals, men of lofty erudition). For he (the man of Nazareth) forbade idol-worship and removed the image-deities, and he held the people responsible for the seven commandments, lest they be like the animals of the field; he sought to perfect them with ethical qualities that are much more rigorous even than those of the Law of Moses (as is well known), a policy that was surely just for its own sake, since that is the most direct way to acquire good traits, . . .[4]

None of the articles of faith in the creed of Maimonides deals with the holiness of Jerusalem, as the Holy City, or Palestine; yet the concept that Jerusalem, as the Holy City, and Palestine, as the Holy Land, have a special relation to Israel and its religion is fundamental to all Judaism. Every prayer contains a petition for the welfare of the Holy City and the Holy Land, and it is a basic principle in Judaism that to provide for the settlement of Palestine is to fulfil one of the Biblical commandments. A Jew seeing a Palestinian city in ruins must recite the benediction of bereavement, for every member of the Jewish faith is expected to regard the desolation of the Holy Land as a personal loss.

In the course of the centuries since the destruction of the Jewish community of Palestine, many efforts have been made to resettle considerable numbers of Jews there, to reclaim its arable land, and to restore some of its ancient forests. Within recent decades, the increased persecution of the Jews in certain countries has made the resettlement of Palestine a matter of practical importance, as well as religious significance. The difficulty encountered in observing certain aspects of Judaism in other countries has also stimulated many to return to Palestine. As a result, there has developed in the Holy Land a community of about 600,000 Jews at the present time (1945).

4 From Jacob Emden's Letter in his edition of *Seder Olam Rabba we-Sutta u-Megillath Taanith*, Hamburg, 1757. A translation of the whole text is given by Oscar Z. Fasman in "An Epistle on Tolerance by a 'Rabbinic Zealot'", in *Judaism in a Changing World*, ed. Rabbi Leo Jung, New York, 1939, pp. 121-136.

In this restored Palestinian community, Hebrew has once more become a spoken language. Hebrew literature flourishes; there has been a rapid development of Hebrew poetry and prose, a greatly stimulated interest in the study of the Holy Scriptures, the Talmud, and later Jewish literature. A considerable portion of the new settlers has devoted itself to agricultural pursuits and lives in "colonies." Many of these are situated in lands which have been reclaimed from the pestilential marshes which covered them since the Arabic conquest, and perhaps for generations before.

In 1917, the British government issued its famous Balfour Declaration, stating that, "His Majesty's Government view with favor the establishment in Palestine of a national home for the Jewish people." This Declaration was subsequently incorporated into the mandate for Palestine, given by the League of Nations to Great Britain. Under the terms of this mandate, the Jewish community in Palestine has enjoyed a certain degree of autonomy, enabling it to regulate in part its own educational system, as well as to administer certain aspects of Talmudic civil law. One of the results of the development of the new settlement in Palestine has been the creation of the Hebrew University in Jerusalem in which the language of instruction is Hebrew.

The sporadic efforts at a renascence of Hebrew as a living tongue, which had been made in different parts of the world during the past century, have received a great impetus from the developments in the Holy Land. At the present time, Hebrew is taught as a spoken language in a considerable number of Jewish communities in all parts of the world.

The group among the Jews who have been most active

in the development of Palestinian life are called Zionists. Among the Zionists, those who are especially interested in reestablishing Palestine as a center of Jewish religious life are called the *Mizrachi* (of the east). Many Jews who are not Zionists also regard the development in Palestine with much sympathy and hope. These are Jews who are convinced that the development of a flourishing Jewish community in Palestine might become an important contribution to the development of human life. These men point, for example, to the interesting manner in which men and women trained in European university life have returned to the simple life of agricultural settlements, finding full satisfaction in the sense of creation which this return has given them. Some of the experiments in communal life now being conducted in Palestine may have significance for other parts of the world.

The complexity of modern life has persuaded a considerable number of Zionists that the future of the Palestinian community and its full usefulness to the development of civilization, will be impeded unless that community has a far greater degree of self-government than it now enjoys. The political status of the Palestinian Jewish community has thus become a matter of discussion, both among Jews and between Jewish groups and the mandatory government. At the present time (October 1945), it is impossible to forecast the result of these discussions.

V. THE SYSTEM OF BLESSINGS

The fundamental concept of the Jewish ceremonial system is that God continually reveals Himself in nature, in history, and in man's daily life. Each ceremony seeks to emphasize some aspect of this Divine revelation, and thus becomes a special means for communion between man and God. By stressing the common dependence of all men on God, ceremonies strengthen the sense of human kinship. By drawing attention to the phenomena of Nature, they help develop man's sense of the esthetic, and increase his joy in the contemplation of beauty. By opening up vistas of achievement and satisfaction, they help free him from subjection to material needs and desires, and enable him to fulfil his higher potentialities.

Jewish tradition has evolved the system of ritual blessings as an effective means for achieving continual realization of God's manifestation in the world. According to rabbinic Law, a Jew is expected to recite a blessing whenever he enjoys any particular aspect of the world. When he awakes, he thanks God for having created the day, for having granted him the power of sight, for the creation of the earth, for the gift of clothes, for the power to walk, and for the renewal of his strength in sleep. He also thanks God that he is not an idolator nor a slave. Mindful of the severity of woman's lot in the world, and her consequent inability to fulfil many of the commandments, the man recites a benediction that he is male, rather than female;

while a woman thanks God that He "has created her according to His will." The observant Jew also recites some verses from Scripture and a passage from the Talmud. Before doing so, he thanks God for the revelation through the Law, and for the commandment to study the Law.

Before sitting down to his morning meal, he is expected to recite the prayers described below. At the meal itself, both before and after eating, he recites prescribed blessings. These blessings are repeated at every meal. The blessing at the beginning of the meal is the simple benediction, "Blessed art Thou, O Lord, our God, King of the Universe, Who dost bring bread out of the ground." The blessing after the meal consists of four paragraphs. The first is devoted to thanks to God for supplying all men and indeed all living things with their daily needs. The second is an expression of gratitude for His having caused ancient Israel to inherit the Holy Land. The third is a prayer for the restoration of Jerusalem. The fourth paragraph is a blessing of God for His continued goodness to all men.

When three people eat together, the blessing after the meal is recited in unison. Such a group is popularly called *mezuman* (prepared), because before he begins, the person reciting the grace asks whether all are prepared for it. If there is a guest at the table, the recital of the grace is assigned to him. If there are several guests, the most learned is expected to recite it. At the end of the grace, the person reciting it invokes a blessing on his host and hostess: "May the All-merciful bless the master and mistress of this house, them, and their house, and their children, and all that is theirs; us, and all that is ours, as our ancestors, Abraham, Isaac, and Jacob were blessed."

At every meal which is attended by three or more people, "words of the Torah" should be spoken. If this is done, the meal becomes sanctified, and "it is as though they have partaken of the table of the Lord," i.e., of a sacrificial meal. In order to fulfil this requirement, it is customary to recite a psalm at every meal. Psalm 137 is recited on weekdays, and Psalm 126 on Sabbaths, festivals, and half-holidays. On festival occasions, and other occasions when it is possible, the recital of these psalms is supplemented by discussions of questions related to religious or spiritual life. To emphasize the sacred character of the meal, it is considered proper to wash one's hands both before and after it, just as was done at sacrificial meals in the Temple.

In addition to these blessings which are recited virtually every day, there are special blessings to be repeated, such as those for the sight of the trees in the spring, a view of the ocean, a meeting with a friend after a long absence, the appearance of meteors, lightning, the rainbow, the new moon, the sight of strange creatures, the acquisition of new clothes,[5] the acquisition of new possessions, and the reception of good news. On hearing bad news, a special benediction must be recited, accepting the Divine judgment. This benediction, "Blessed art Thou, O Lord our God, King of the Universe, the true Judge," is also recited on the occasion of any bereavement. Finally, there are prayers prescribed for the afternoon and the evening (see below) and a concluding prayer at bedtime.

[5] This blessing is not recited when wearing leather garments because it is not considered fitting to thank God for life when using material produced at the cost of life.

VI. THE SYNAGOGUE AND THE PRAYERS

In ancient times, the center of Jewish worship was at the Temple in Jerusalem, where sacrifices were offered in accordance with the prescriptions of the Law. But there were prophets in Israel even in the days of priests, and the prophets frequently organized prayer-meetings at which people assembled for devotion and religious exhortation. From these meetings eventually the synagogue was to develop; and subsequently the church and the mosque. As the chief element in the Temple service was sacrifice, so that of the synagogue was prayer. The precedent for prayer was, of course, an ancient one. Abraham interceded with God on behalf of the people of Sodom. Fearing attack, Jacob uttered the beautiful prayer which contains the memorable words, "I am not worthy of all the mercies, and of all the truth, which Thou hast shown Thy servant; for with my staff I passed this Jordan, and now I am become two camps" (Genesis 32.11). Hannah came to the Temple to petition and praise the Lord. Indeed, Solomon in his dedication service referred to the Temple essentially as a house of prayer in which men would supplicate the Lord.

Even before the Exile, gatherings for prayer were to be found among the people. The Babylonian exile and the return to Palestine, however, were especially instrumental in strengthening the synagogue. The institution offered not only an opportunity for pious devotion but for study as well, for it was at these assemblies that Scripture was read and explained. The assembly for worship which proved of such importance in Palestine while the Temple at Jerusalem still endured, became indispensable when the Temple was destroyed. Since that time, the synagogue has been the sole sanctuary of the Jewish people.

The architecture of the synagogue varies according to country and age. The essential elements of the institution are the Ark containing the scroll of the Law, a stand for the reader of the service who faces the Ark, and in most traditional synagogues a second stand in the middle of the gathering for the reading of the Law. In a large number of American synagogues, no provision is made for this second stand.

In accordance with the tradition derived from the Temple in Jerusalem, the "court of women" is separated from that of the men in traditional synagogues. It is either marked off by a partition, or is situated in a gallery. Again, a considerable number of American synagogues, including most of the conservative synagogues and all the reform synagogues, have deviated from tradition in this respect, and permit men and women to sit together.

No human figures may be used in the decoration of the synagogue. However, it is permitted, and has even become customary, to depict on the Ark and elsewhere in the building a lion or an eagle, suggesting the latter half of the rabbinical injunction, "Be bold as the leopard, fleet as the deer, light as the eagle, and strong as the lion, to do the will of thy Father who is in Heaven." In many synagogues, the passage is inscribed over the reader's stand. It is also usual to place over the Ark a symbolic representation of the two tablets containing the Ten Commandments. Generally, only the first words of each of the

Commandments is inscribed on the tablets. The so-called Shield (or Star) of David which is found in many synagogue buildings, and otherwise in Jewish symbolism, is of unknown origin. But its use can be traced back to rabbinic times.

In many synagogues, there is to be found over the reader's desk a candelabrum, or two candelabra, symbolic of that which stood in the Temple of Jerusalem. But because it is forbidden to set up in a synagogue an exact replica of the utensils used in the ancient Temple, such candelabra usually have instead of seven, eight or nine, sometimes fourteen branches.

In further deference to the unique sanctity of the Temple, kneeling or prostrating oneself in the synagogue worship is forbidden, except on special occasions in the services of the New Year's Day and the Day of Atonement. Prayers are said either standing or sitting. It is customary to bow one's head on entering the synagogue, and while reciting certain portions of the prayers. In orthodox and conservative synagogues, men pray with covered heads. It is considered a violation of custom to perform any act of worship, including study of the Scripture or the Talmud, with uncovered head. This custom derives from that prescribed for the priests of the Temple in Exodus 28.40-42. The custom has been abandoned in most American reform synagogues.

It has become customary to speak of reform synagogues and conservative synagogues, as Temples. This change of name does not imply any difference other than those already indicated.

The essential element in the synagogue is, of course, not the building, but the community. Public worship may be conducted in a building, or out of doors. But it can be held only in the presence of a congregation, which theoretically consists of a minimum of ten heads of households. For the purpose of prayer, and because of the difficulty in finding ten heads of households in very small communities, ten males (over thirteen years of age) are considered heads of households. The assembly of ten such people is called a *minyan* (quorum) sufficient for public service.

Any adult male Jew may lead the congregation in public prayers. The rabbi participates simply as a member of the congregation. It has become usual in large congregations to appoint a special official to read the prayers, especially those of the Sabbaths and festivals. Such a reader is called a *hazzan.* In some congregations the *hazzan* has a choir to assist him. In orthodox congregations, this choir consists only of men; in some conservative and in all reform congregations, women are also admitted to the choir. A number of passages in the service are traditionally sung by the whole congregation in unison. The tendency of modern orthodox and conservative synagogues is to extend this practice to include a much larger part of the service.

In addition to the *hazzan,* the congregation may require the services of a special reader for the Scriptures. He must be able not only to read the consonantal text of the scroll without the aid of vowels, but must be expert in the traditional system of cantillation of the Scriptures. This system of chanting is of great historical interest, because at least certain parts of it, particularly that prescribed for use on the High Holy Days, are obviously of great antiquity.

The duty of looking after the arrangements for the service, that is, seeing that the scrolls are prepared for reading, that the prayer-books are available for the worshippers, and that the members having special duties during the service know their assignments, devolves generally on a functionary called the *shammash* (sexton).

In addition to these officials who generally are remunerated for their duties, American congregations usually have lay officers, a president, one or more vice-presidents, a secretary, a treasurer, and board of directors, upon whom devolves the responsibility for the material well-being of the congregation.

As already indicated, tradition expects every member of the Jewish faith to pray at least three times a day: in the morning, *shaharit;* in the afternoon, *minhah;* and in the evening, *ma'arib*. On Sabbaths and festivals, an additional prayer is assigned for morning service, called *musaf* (addition), to commemorate the special sacrifices which were offered on such days at the Temple in Jerusalem. On the Day of Atonement, a fifth prayer is recited at sunset. This prayer, in some respects the most solemn of the year, is called *ne'ilah* (closing), and commemorates the service held at the Temple when its gates were closed at the end of the sacred day.

All of these prayers should, so far as possible, be recited at a public service. But if it is difficult to arrange to participate in a public service, they can be recited in private (with omissions of certain portions which belong only to the public service). Most observant Jews attend synagogue services at least on the Sabbaths and holidays; every orthodox and conservative synagogue endeavors to arrange for public services also on weekdays.

The essential element in all these services is the prayer called *'amidah* (literally, standing, so called because one must rise to recite it). The weekday version of this prayer consists of nineteen paragraphs. But in the original Palestinian form, given it by Rabban Gamaliel II eighteen centuries ago, it contained only eighteen paragraphs; and the prayer is therefore frequently called *shemoneh 'esreh* (eighteen).

At all services, except the evening service, this prayer is recited twice. It is first recited in an undertone by each individual in the congregation; and then aloud by the reader, on behalf of the congregation. The first and last three paragraphs of the *'amidah* are identical for all the services. The first paragraphs consist of confessions of faith in God as the God of the Patriarchs, Abraham, Isaac, and Jacob; as the One Who gives strength to the living and new life to the dead; and as the Holy One, Who has no equal. The final paragraphs include a prayer for the return of God's presence to Jerusalem; an expression of gratitude for all the goodness God has shown us; and a prayer for peace.

On the festivals, it is the rule in all orthodox and in many conservative synagogues, that the descendants of the ancient Aaronid priests bless the people before the final paragraphs of the public reading of the *musaf 'amidah.* The formula used in this blessing is that prescribed in Numbers 6.22-27, "May the Lord bless thee and keep thee; may the Lord cause His countenance to shine upon thee and be gracious unto thee; may the Lord lift His countenance upon thee and give thee peace."

Before reciting this blessing, the descendants of Aaron who are in the synagogue, remove their shoes (as was the custom in the Temple in Jerusalem). The Levites who are present in the synagogue then wash the hands of the Aaronids, who thereupon step forward, face the congregation, and recite the ancient blessing.

The middle paragraphs of the daily *'amidah* contain

petitions for the fulfilment of various needs for the granting of wisdom, repentance, and forgiveness, for the redemption of Israel, for the healing of the sick, for prosperous years, for the gathering of the dispersed, for the restoration of the Sanhedrin, for the suppression of tyranny, for the protection of the righteous, for the rebuilding of Jerusalem, for the coming of the Messiah, and for the acceptance of prayer.

All of the prayers are for the good of the whole community. Petitions for private needs may be inserted in their appropriate place. For example, the prayer for a sick person may be included in the general prayer for the sick of the world.

On Sabbaths and festivals, these petitions for the satisfaction of material wants are necessarily omitted; for it is forbidden to consider material needs on such days. On these occasions there is a single prayer for a complete rest on the Sabbath, and for happiness on the festival.

At every service the silent reading of the *'amidah* ends with the prayer which begins: "O, my God! Guard my tongue from evil, and my lips from speaking guile. To such as curse me, let me be dumb. Let me, indeed, be as dust unto all. . . . If any design evil against me, speedily make their counsel of no effect, and frustrate their intentions."

At the morning and evening services the *'amidah* is preceded by the recital of the *Shema* and the various benedictions with it. The *Shema* begins with the verse, "Hear, O Israel, the Lord is our God, the Lord is One" (Deuteronomy 6.4), and includes Deuteronomy 6.5-9, 11.13-21, and Numbers 15.37-41. In all services the recital of the *Shema* is preceded by a blessing of God for His revelation in the Law, and is followed by a blessing for His redemption of Israel from Egypt. In the morning, there is also a blessing for the light, in the evening a blessing for the darkness.

Each of the services begins and ends with the recital of the *Kaddish,* an Aramaic prayer for the coming of the Kingdom of God. It is, in effect, a prayer on behalf of the congregation by the reader before he enters on his service and after he ends it. Its essential element is its first section, reading: "May the great Name of God be exalted and sanctified in the world which He created according to His will, and may He cause His Kingdom to come, in your lives and in your days, and in the lives of all the House of Israel; speedily, and in a short time. Amen."

In the course of time, it has become customary to recite this prayer also at other parts of the service. Since the Middle Ages, it has been usual also to recite it during the year of a bereavement, and on the anniversary of the death of one's parents.

In the morning services held on Mondays and Thursdays (the market days of ancient Palestine, when a larger congregation would be available than on other weekdays), as well as on Sabbaths, festivals, new moons, and fast days, portions of the Five Books of Moses are read from the sacred scrolls. The readings are so arranged that the whole of the Pentateuch is covered within a year. On Sabbath and festival mornings, as well as at the afternoon services on fast days, selections from the Books of the Prophets are read in addition to those from the Torah. Such a portion is called the *haftarah,* and the person reading it is called the *maftir.*

As stated above, the reading from the Torah is now assigned to a special functionary. In ancient times, the members of the congregation would each ascend in turn to perform this duty. In deference to this tradition, it is still customary to call various individuals to read special portions of the Torah, though they merely repeat the words *sotto voce,* while the reading aloud is the duty of the professional reader. There are seven such participants in the Sabbath morning reading of the Torah; six in that of the Day of Atonement, five in those of the festivals; four in those of new moons and the festival weeks; and three at all other services when the Torah is read. Whenever the Torah is read, the first person to be called must be a descendant of Aaron, if there is any in the synagogue. The second to be called must be a Levite, and the others are chosen from the remainder of the congregation. When the prophetic portions are read at morning services of the Sabbaths and festivals, an additional person is called. He may be either an Aaronid, a Levite, or any other Israelite.

There are certain occasions when it is considered an especial obligation to participate in the public reading of the Torah. The most important of these are the Sabbath succeeding one's thirteenth birthday (see below); the Sabbath preceding one's marriage; the anniversaries of the death of one's parents; and the Sabbath following one's recovery from illness or escape from danger. It is usual for persons who are thus required to participate in the reading of the Scriptures, to be assigned to the *haftarah.* A person who reads the Torah after recovering from illness or escape from danger, recites a special blessing on the occasion, saying: "Blessed be Thou, O Lord, our God, King of the Universe, Who dost grant kindness to the undeserving, and Who hast granted me every good." The congregation, hearing the blessing, responds, "He Who has granted thee kindness, may He ever continue to grant thee kindness."

The language of the prayers of the traditional service is for the most part Hebrew. However, a number of prayers are in Aramaic which was the vernacular of the Jews in the first centuries of the Christian era in Palestine and Babylonia. At the present time the proportion of Hebrew to some other language (in America, for example, English) will vary with the individual congregation. But everywhere some portions of the public service are read in Hebrew.

According to rabbinic tradition, it is customary for men to wear a prayer-shawl called the *tallit* (garment) during the morning prayers. This prayer-shawl is a square or oblong woolen cloth, with fringe at each of its four corners. It is a very ancient garment, probably worn in antiquity as a cloak. The purpose of the fringe (*ṣiṣit*) at the four corners is explained in the Bible: "That ye may look upon it and remember all the commandments of the Lord and do them . . . and be holy unto the Lord your God" (Numbers 15.39-40). In addition, it is customary for men to don the *tephillin* (phylacteries) during the morning services on weekdays. These *tephillin* consist of two boxes of parchment to which are attached long leather straps. In the boxes are deposited little strips of parchment with the contents of Exodus 11.16, 13.1-10; Deuteronomy 6.4-9, 11.13-21. The Bible also gives the meaning of this symbol: "And it shall be for a sign unto thee upon thy hand, and for a memorial between thine eyes, that the Law of the Lord may be in thy mouth; for with a strong hand hath the Lord brought thee out of Egypt" (Exodus 13.9). To the ancient rabbis the *tephillin* on the head, and on the left arm close to the heart, represented the concentration of the intellect and the emotion on the Divine. As Maimonides subsequently expressed it: "As long as the *tephil-*

lin are on the head and on the arm of a man, he is modest and God-fearing; he will not be attracted by hilarity or idle talk, and will have no evil thoughts, but will devote all his thoughts to truth and righteousness."

Two of these Biblical sections, namely Deuteronomy 6.4-9 and 11.13-21, are also inscribed on pieces of parchment which are placed in receptacles, attached by the observant Jew to the doorposts of every room. Such receptacles are called *mezuzot* (literally, doorposts). These inscriptions are intended to remind man, as he enters home or leaves it, of the unity of God and of the duty of loving Him.

VII. THE SABBATH AND THE FESTIVALS

While according to the Jewish faith God's presence can be felt at any time and place, there are times, just as there are places, which through their associations have become especially propitious for communion with God. Of these the most important are the holy days and the fast days. The holy days, according to the Jewish ritual, are the *Shabbat* or Sabbath, celebrated on the seventh day of each week, *Pesach* (Passover), *Shabuot* (Pentecost), *Rosh Ha-Shanah* (the Jewish religious New Year's Day), *Yom Kippur* (Day of Atonement), and *Sukkot* (Tabernacles).

In order that these days may be devoted as completely as possible to the spiritual life, work is forbidden on them. This prohibition includes not only all gainful occupation, but also household tasks.

As a result of these various prohibitions, the Sabbath and festivals become virtually periods of cessation of all labor on the part of observant Jews. Because of the difficulties involved in maintaining this rigid discipline in an industrial society like our own, many Jews otherwise very observant, do not refrain from all labor on the Sabbath. Nevertheless, even among these a large number set aside the free hours of the day for spiritual contemplation and for prayer, and mark the Sabbath with the ceremonials devoted to it.

Theoretically, observant Jews should not benefit from the willingness of members of other faiths to perform tasks for them on the Sabbath day. But because of the severity of the winters in Northern and Central Europe, and the consequent danger of disease, it became customary in the Middle Ages to permit people who were not Jews to kindle the fire for the Jews on the Sabbath. As a result, in time Christian and Moslem boys came to look after the heating of Jewish homes on the Sabbath. In recent centuries, people of other faiths also extinguish lights for Jews on the Sabbath, on the theory that rest is as imperative for health as warmth.

In the Jewish religious calendar, the observance of festivals begins a little before sunset on the preceding day. Because no fire is kindled on the Sabbath, it has been customary from time immemorial for Jewish housewives to conclude all their household arrangements for the day of rest by preparing the lights, which have therefore become known as the "Sabbath lights." The great antiquity of this usage, and the significance which came to be attached to it, have sanctified it, and consequently in modern Jewish homes the Sabbath candles are lit, even though other means of illumination are available and are in use. Many a Jew has tender memories of the sight of his mother lighting the Sabbath candles. As their light is not to be enjoyed before the blessing, the Jewish mother with her hands over her eyes recites, "Blessed are Thou, O Lord our God, King of the Universe, Who has sanctified us with Thy commandments, and commanded us to kindle the Sabbath lights."

In the absence of the mother of the household, the lights are kindled by someone acting for her. If by chance the lights have not been kindled on a Sabbath, it is customary for her to kindle an additional light before every Sabbath afterward throughout her life.

The beauty and impressiveness of the custom of the Sabbath lights has caused it to be extended, so that similar lights are now kindled also on festivals for which the use of fire is permitted, and therefore there is no special reason for lighting candles before dark. In kindling the lights on the seasonal festivals, however, the mother recites the special prayer of thanks for life called *sheheheyanu* (Who has kept us alive), "Blessed art Thou, O Lord our God, King of the Universe, Who hast caused us to live, and attain this day."

Evening services are held in the synagogue on the eve of festivals and Sabbaths at dusk. After the services, the members of the family return home for the Sabbath meal. On the table are placed a flask of wine and two loaves of bread. The Sabbath loaf of bread is called by its Hebrew name, *hallah* (plural, *hallot,* or as popularly pronounced, *hallos*). The two loaves of bread are said to symbolize the double share of manna which God granted the Israelites in the wilderness on Fridays to provide for the Sabbath (Exodus 16.5). It is customary in many localities to prepare these loaves in an especially attractive form, made of twisted strands of dough. On festivals, the bread is further enriched by a plentiful supply of raisins. (On Passover, as will be seen below, the bread is replaced by unleavened cakes.) The loaves of bread are covered with a napkin, and the head of the household takes a cup of wine, and recites over it the blessing called the *kiddush,* or sanctification of the day. This blessing consists of a prayer of thanks to God for the gift of the wine, and then for the gift of the special festival. The head of the household drinks some of the wine, and distributes the rest among the others present. On seasonal festivals, the *kiddush* also includes the blessing *sheheheyanu,* mentioned above. Then follows the ritual washing of the hands, the blessing for the bread, the breaking of the bread, the meal itself, the special hymns of the Sabbath or the festival meal, and the blessing after the meal.

In many conservative and reform congregations, special services on Sabbath eve are held after the Sabbath meal. These services are intended to enable those men and women who because of modern industrial conditions do not attend the traditional service at dusk, to commune with God during the course of the holy day. The ritual used at these services varies considerably. In some congregations, it is the usual Sabbath eve service. In others, it consists ot the hymns sung at the Sabbath evening meal. In virtually all congregations where such services are held, it is customary to include a sermon by the rabbi.

The Sabbath and festival morning service are longer than those of the weekdays, and occupy most of the morning hours. As it is considered improper to eat before prayers, traditional Jewish homes do not provide for any breakfast on Sabbaths or festivals. The ritual of the noon meal is very similar to that of the evening. It includes a blessing over the cup of wine, the blessing for the bread, the breaking and distribution of the bread, the meal itself, and the blessing after the meal.

It is customary in observant homes to arrange for another meal to be served in the late afternoon of the Sabbath day, so as to complete three Sabbath meals. This third meal is called *seudah shelishit* (third meal), or more popularly and less correctly, *shalosh seudot* (three meals). No wine need be drunk before the third meal, but the blessing for the bread is recited as usual.

In Palestine, it has become customary within the last decade, as a result of the influence of the famous Hebrew poet, Chayyim Nahman Bialik, to substitute for the third meal, a public gathering, preferably one at which refreshments are served, called *oneg shabbat,* the delight of the Sabbath. The practice of holding such gatherings has become an institution in other parts of the world, and is rapidly being adopted by congregations in this country. It is an effort to bring people together on the Sabbath afternoon for a discussion of religious, literary, or ethical problems, while participating in a symbolic Sabbath meal.

The Sabbath is concluded after sunset with a blessing called *habdalah* (division, that is, marking the division between the Sabbath and the weekdays). A flask of wine and a box of incense are set on the table, and a light is struck. It seems appropriate that the workaday week should begin with the taste of the wine, the odor of the incense, and the appearance of the light, which, satisfying three different senses, increase man's awareness of his dependence on God for all his needs. The blessing consists, therefore, of thanks to God for the gift of the wine, of the incense, and of the light; and ends with further thanks for the division between the Sabbath and the weekdays. It is customary to let the cup of wine for *habdalah* overflow, as a symbol that the happiness of the week may likewise overflow. It is also customary to use a candle with three or four wicks (resembling an ancient torch) for the light of the *habdalah.*

The same ritual of *habdalah* is recited in the synagogue, in order to provide for those who cannot observe it in their homes. It also concludes the Day of Atonement, and with the exception of the blessing for the light, all the other festivals.

The rigid prohibition of work on the Sabbath does not, as is frequently believed, make it a day of gloom for the observant Jew. On the contrary, the complete release from all mundane concern, the concentration on the study of the Torah, and the joy in the sense of communion with God, make it a day of great, though perhaps indescribable, delight. To participate in the observance of the Sabbath gives such happiness, that one of the prayers added to the blessing after the meal on the day, asks that Paradise may be one long Sabbath. As twilight descends on Sabbath afternoon, some feel an ineffable sense of yearning and lonesomeness, which the mystics among the Jews have characterized as the loss of part of one's soul.

Aside from the Sabbath, the major Jewish festivals are Passover, Pentecost, New Year's Day, the Day of Atonement, and the Feast of the Tabernacles. Each of these is according to tradition a day of judgment for all mankind. "On Passover the world is judged regarding its grain; on Pentecost regarding the fruits of the tree; on New Year's Day (and also on the Day of Atonement) all creatures pass before God as in a military review; and on Tabernacles they are judged concerning the rain."

While this consciousness of judgment gives an air of solemnity to all the festivals, the three festivals of the ancient pilgrimages, Passover, Pentecost, and Tabernacles, are primarily periods of joy. The manner in which the joy of the festival is combined with the sense of solemnity and judgment before God is difficult to explain to the uninitiate. The festival prayers, as well as the special melodies which in certain rituals accompany them, reflect a feeling of awe, arising from the sense of communion with God as Judge and Ruler of the universe; yet united with this feeling and permeating it, is a sense of confidence that His judgment will be one of mercy rather than severity, as that of a father upon his child. The joy of the festival is thus prevented from becoming one of physical pleasure or self-indulgence. Ideally conceived, it is a joy arising largely from participation in synagogue and home rituals, which bring about a closer communion with God.

The significance of each festival is enhanced through the natural and historical interpretations associated with it. All of them are intended to increase man's faith in God by reference to His revelation in the natural order, and also in the succession of human events. Their symbols are particularly significant in an industrial and commercial civilization, where man tends to be separated from nature; and their reflection of the Divine purpose in history gives one strength in times of international crisis, and fills one with humility in moments of peace and prosperity. The purpose of the festivals may thus be said to place human life in both its cosmic and historical perspectives. They enable Man to see himself both as part of Nature and as distinguished through the providence of God.

Passover, occurring on the full moon of the first month of spring (toward the end of March or the beginning of April), is the great festival of the re-birth of Nature, and also commemorates historically the exodus from Egypt. The concentration of Jews in the cities during past centuries has tended to minimize the agricultural aspect of the Passover. Nevertheless, certain ancient customs emphasizing the seasonal character of the festival are still observed. The first month of spring in Palestine marks the end of the rainy season and the beginning of the dry season. In this dry season, the crops are saved from destruction by a heavy dew each night. Hence Passover has become a festival of prayer for the dew, and the *musaf* (additional) prayer of the first day of Passover is dedicated to petition for copious dew on the earth. The second night of Passover was celebrated in ancient Palestine as the beginning of the barley harvest. In accordance with Leviticus 23.14, no part of the new crop might be eaten before that night, when the first sheaf was harvested and prepared as a sacrifice to God. While the observance of the sacrifice is impossible today, it is still customary for men of great piety in European communities to avoid eating the new grain before the second night of Passover. All traditional Jewish communities mark the second night of Passover as the beginning of the barley harvest in ancient Palestine; and following a literal interpretation of Leviticus 23.15-16, include in the daily evening service, an enumeration of the forty-nine days from that night until Pentecost, the festival of the wheat harvest.

But the historical significance of Passover as commemorating the Exodus and the promulgation of the idea of freedom in the world, has far overshadowed the agricultural phase of the festival. The ceremonies prescribed for the festival in Scripture and the additional rules established by the rabbis, have as their purpose emphasis on the idea of human liberty and equality. The most obvious characteristic of the festival is the use of the unleavened bread (called *maṣṣah,* pronounced *matzah*), the bread of affliction (Deuteronomy 16.3), recalling to each Jew, the bondage of his ancestry in Egypt, and emphasizing by inference his equality with the humblest and most oppressed of men. The significance of the custom has become such that it is observed with greater precision than almost any other law in Scripture. Observant Jews abstain from eating not only any leavened bread on the festival, but even any food which might conceivably have a taste or trace of leaven. The grain used for *maṣṣah* is carefully examined to see whether any of it has become leaven. The examination is usually performed by a rabbi, who takes a sampling of the grain. If he finds that none of those in his sample has become leaven, the contents of that granary may be used for Passover. After the examination, the grain must be carefully guarded against any moistening, which might cause it to leaven. The mills in which it is ground are carefully scoured and purified from all leaven. The flour is then again guarded against moisture, until it is brought to the bakery. In the bakery, expert mechanics and especially devised machines make it possible to prepare the dough and bake it with such speed that it is quite impossible for any leavening to take place. No salt, and of course no yeast or any material other than flour and water, enter into the making of the *maṣṣah*. After the *maṣṣah* has been baked, it may be ground again into flour, which can then be used for making pastries and other dishes for consumption on the Passover. Such flour is called *matzah meal.*

Traditional observance of the Passover requires that no prepared food such as dried fruits or vegetables shall be used, unless it has been made certain that not a speck of flour attaches to them. For this reason, raisins, prunes, coffee, pepper, and similar foods are used by observant Jews during the Passover only if they are prepared under the supervision of a rabbi. Dried peas or beans may not be eaten under any circumstances. Ashkenazic Jews do not eat rice on Passover, though following the tradition of their ancestors, Jews of Sephardic descent consider it permitted.

Special cooking utensils and dishes are set aside for the Passover week, so that no utensils or dishes which have contained leaven will come into contact with the Passover food. Families which cannot afford a complete set of special dishes may cleanse their metal utensils and certain types of glassware for use during the Passover week. Such cleansing must follow the ritual prescriptions, and should be done only after consultation with a rabbi.

To purify the home from all leaven before the Passover, it is customary on the night before the festival eve to "search the house" for any bread or leaven. In earlier ages, this searching had the practical purpose of discovering such leaven, for in the simple one-room homes of the ancient east it was possible to delay the removal of leaven until the night before the festival. In modern homes, this cleaning naturally occupies several days or even weeks, and the ritual searching for the leaven is virtually a formal custom. Nevertheless, the custom is observed in most orthodox and conservative homes. The head of the household searches for the leaven, removes all he finds, and puts it aside until the next morning, when it must be burned during the first quarter of the day, that is, around 9:00 a.m. After that hour it is forbidden to eat leavened food or to own it. As it is usually difficult to destroy all the leavened food in a home and quite impossible to dispose of all the dishes used for leavened food, it is customary among many groups of observant Jews to transfer the title of their leavened food to the rabbi of the community during the Passover week. The rabbi in turn technically transfers the title to this food to a member of another faith.

On the first and second nights of Passover, a unique home service is celebrated. This celebration is called the *seder* (order), because the whole meal follows a prescribed ritual order. There is a festive gathering of the whole family in each household, and strangers who are separated from their families are invited as guests. In communities where the number of strangers is considerable, provision is frequently made for a group *seder* at a public institution.

The poignant beauty of the *seder* service leaves an indelible impression on every Jewish child who participates in it. It is in effect a pageant in which ancient Palestinian life is recreated in as detailed and precise a form as possible. The head of the household (or at a public celebration, the leader of the service) is provided with a divan on which after the fashion of the ancients, he may recline during the meal and the celebration. According to some rituals, he is expected to don a *kittel,* a white linen garment worn in ancient Jerusalem on festive days.

The service followed at the *seder* is described in a special prayer-book, the *Passover Haggadah.* This book contains directions for arranging the Passover dish to be placed before the master of the house, and detailed instructions for the procedure during the service.

One of the most significant elements in the *seder* is its highly developed pedagogical technique. In order to impress the child, he is urged to observe the various ceremonies which are conducted, and to ask for an explanation of them. As the service is recited it thus becomes fundamentally a reply to these questions. The child is informed that the celebration is in memory of the Exodus from Egypt; he is told the story of the Israelite bondage; of the redemption of the people through the mercy of God; and is taught to respect the liberty which he has inherited through this redemption.

At the end of the Passover meal, which is eaten in the course of the *seder,* the door is opened as a symbol of the entry of Elijah the Prophet. A cup of wine, "the cup of Elijah," is filled, the whole company rise, and cry, "Blessed is he who has come!" The concept that Elijah, the immortal prophet, visits every Jewish home on the Passover eve, emphasizes the significance of the festival as a symbol of eternal freedom, as well as memorial of a past emancipation; for Elijah is the prophet who, according to the words of Malachi, will be the precursor of God's establishing His Kingdom on earth, at the end of days.

The *seder* ends with the recital of various psalms, the tasting of a fourth and final cup of wine, the singing of various hymns, and finally with popular songs, dating from mediaeval times. In many communities, the head of the household concludes the whole service by reading the Biblical Book, Canticles (The Song of Songs). The joyful spirit of youth, which permeates that book, seems appropriate for the spring festival; and the allegorical meaning imposed on it, as an epic of God's relation to Israel, are particularly fitting for recollection on the festival of the Exodus.

The period between Passover and Pentecost is now observed in many Jewish communities as one of partial mourning, because it is traditionally described as the time when the disciples of Rabbi Akiba, one of the foremost teachers of the Talmud, died. Except for certain special days within the period, no weddings are celebrated by observant Jews; and they also abstain from listening to music, attending theatres, or participating in other pleasures.

The thirty-third day of this period, called *Lag Ba'Omer* (literally, the thirty-third day of the *Omer*), is a half-holiday, devoted to the celebration of weddings and other festivities. It is sometimes said to be the anniversary of the death of Rabbi Simeon ben Yohai, the foremost of Rabbi Akiba's disciples, which is marked in this way as the occasion of his translation to the Heavenly Academy. To this day it is therefore customary in Palestine to mark the day with a festive pilgrimage to the supposed grave of Rabbi Simeon in Meron, a village of Galilee.

Pentecost or *Shabuot* (occurring toward the end of May or the beginning of June) is described in Scripture primarily as the festival of the wheat harvest (Exodus 23.16). But it also commemorates the Revelation on Mount Sinai, and is therefore the festival of the Ten Commandments. The reading of the Law assigned to it covers the chapter telling the story of the Revelation (Exodus 19.20); the liturgy of the day is also dedicated in part to commemorating this incident. In many orthodox congregations, the evening of the first night of Pentecost is spent in reading Scriptural passages. Among some especially pious Jews, it is customary to remain awake all night, reading the Bible and the Talmud. In many modern congregations, the first day of Pentecost is celebrated by the confirmation of boys and girls, a ceremony which is described in greater detail, below.

The third of the great joyous festivals is that of Tabernacles or *Sukkot,* marking the coming of the autumn and the late harvests (some time in October), and also commemorating God's protection during the period when Israel dwelt in the wilderness (Leviticus 23.43).

Both the seasonal and the historical aspects of the festival are symbolized in the *sukkah,* the booth in which observant Jews eat their meals during the holiday week. This booth is essentially a rustic cabin, with improvised walls, and a covering of leafy branches and twigs instead of a solid roof or ceiling. It is customary to adorn both the covering and the walls with vegetables and fruits, in order to make the harvest rusticity of the surroundings especially clear and emphatic.

The festival is celebrated further by the ceremonial of

the *lulab,* a cluster of a palm branch, three myrtle twigs, and two willow sprigs. During the recital of the *hallel* (i.e., Psalms 113-118) in the morning service of the festival, the *lulab* together with a citron, is taken in hand, and at certain portions of the prayer, they are moved to and fro, eastward, southward, westward, northward, upward, and downward, to indicate that God, Who is being thanked for His gifts, is to be found everywhere. At the end of the service, a scroll is taken out of the Ark, and each of those having a *lulab* marches about the scroll in a festive procession, commemorating the similar procession about the altar in Jerusalem in the days of the Temple.

On the seventh day of *Sukkot* (*Hoshanna Rabba*) there is a special service of prayer for abundant rains. After the usual service of the day, the clusters of palm branches are put down, and clusters of willow taken up (the willow symbolic of abundance of rain, because it grows by the riverside). With these willow clusters in hand, the congregation recites various hymns having the refrain *hoshanna* (or, as it was frequently pronounced in ancient times, *hosanna*) meaning, "Help, we pray Thee." At the end of these hymns, the willows are beaten against the floor of the synagogue.

Following *Hoshanna Rabba,* is the "eighth day of solemn assembly" or, as it is called in Hebrew, *Shemini Aṣeret.* This festival is intended as a climax for the joyful season, which begins with *Sukkot.* The festival is marked especially by the prayer for rain in the additional (*musaf*) service, which is therefore called *tephillat geshem* (the prayer for rain).

The final or ninth day of the autumn celebration (properly the second day of the *Shemini Aṣeret* festival) is popularly called *Simhat Torah* (the day of rejoicing in the

Law). On this day, the last section of the Five Books of Moses, *viz.*, Deuteronomy, chapter 34, as well as the first section of Genesis are read. In celebration of the annual completion and fresh beginning of the reading of the Pentateuch, all the scrolls of the Law are taken from the Ark and carried about the synagogue in a procession. To enable every member of the congregation to participate in this ceremonial, the procession moves about the synagogue hall at least seven times in the evening, and then seven times more at the morning service. It is also customary in certain rituals for each member of the congregation to participate in the public reading of the Pentateuch on *Simhat Torah*. Immediately before the reading of the last section of the Pentateuch, it is customary in most congregations to call to read from the Torah one of the distinguished members of the congregation together "with all the children" (Hebrew, *kol ha-nearim*), so that even minors may participate in the reading on this occasion.

The person called to complete the reading of the Pentateuch on *Simhat Torah* is called *hatan ha-torah* (bridegroom of the Law, popularly pronounced, *hoson torah*). The person called to read the first chapter in Genesis on that day is called *hatan bereshit* (the bridegroom of the beginning, popularly pronounced, *hoson bereshis*). These offices are usually bestowed on men of especial piety or learning, and are among the highest honors which can be given in the synagogue service.

While on these festivals communion with God is sought through joy, on *Rosh Ha-Shanah* and *Yom Kippur* it is sought through solemnity. They are described as Days of Judgment when all living things pass before God, to stand in judgment for their deeds during the past year. During the month before *Rosh Ha-Shanah* (which usually occurs during the last three weeks of September or the beginning of October), preparation is made for the festival by sounding a ram's horn at the synagogue service each morning, and reciting Psalm 27 each morning and evening. Beginning with the Sunday preceding *Rosh Ha-Shanah* (if *Rosh Ha-Shanah* occurs on Monday or Tuesday, beginning with the Sunday of the preceding week), special prayers (called *selihot*) are recited at dawn of each day, beseeching Divine forgiveness for man's transgressions. While only the most pious assemble at the synagogue to recite these prayers each day, many recite them on the first day, and on the day before *Rosh Ha-Shanah.* In some congregations, these prayers are recited at midnight rather than at dawn, to make possible a larger attendance.

The festival of *Rosh Ha-Shanah* itself is particularly devoted to prayers for peace and prosperity for all mankind, and for life and happiness for individual human beings. It also emphasizes the recognition of God as King of the universe. This phase of the festival is reflected not only in the prayers of the day, but in several of the ceremonials. The ram's horn or *shofar* is sounded before, during, and after the additional morning prayer. The notes sounded by the *shofar* tend to arouse the people to repentance, reminding them that the Kingdom of God can be realized in our hearts and in our personal lives, even in the world in which we live. In the afternoon of the first day of the festival, it is customary in many communities to walk to a river bank, as was sometimes done in ancient times at the anointing of a king. This custom of walking to the river bank is called *tashlik* (throwing), because of the popular belief that it is intended to cast off one's sins into the river.

On the evening of the first day of *Rosh Ha-Shanah,* it is

customary to eat apples and other fruits, dipped in honey, saying, "May it be Thy will that this year shall be happy and sweet for us." In many localities, bread is dipped in honey at all the meals eaten on *Rosh Ha-Shanah,* and during the days following it until the Day of Atonement. On the second evening of *Rosh Ha-Shanah,* it is customary to eat new fruit, over which the blessing *sheheheyanu* is recited.

The ten days beginning with the first days of *Rosh Ha-Shanah* and ending with *Yom Kippur,* are called the "Ten Days of Penitence." It is expected that everyone will observe especially high standards of ethical and ceremonial conduct during these days. There are special prayers assigned for the period, beseeching continuance of life and peace, and the *selihot* are recited on them as on the days preceding *Rosh Ha-Shanah.*

On the day preceding *Yom Kippur* (the ninth of *Tishri*) tradition prescribes festive meals. The final meal of the day, eaten before the sundown which ushers in *Yom Kippur,* thus is marked by a peculiar combination of joy and solemnity, which leaves an indelible impression. Before eating this meal, an oral confession of one's sins is recited as part of the afternoon prayer. It is also customary during the day to distribute money for charitable purposes. After the meal, the head of the household kindles a lamp or candle of sufficient size to burn for twenty-four hours, that is, until the end of the day. The mother kindles the usual festival lights, and the family proceeds to the synagogue.

The Day of Atonement is a season not only for repentance for trespasses against the ceremonial law, but more especially for trespasses committed against ethical conduct in relations between men. Forgiveness for these trespasses can only be obtained when the man who suffered wrong pardons the injustice. It is therefore customary for anyone who is conscious of having injured a neighbor, to obtain forgiveness before the Day of Atonement.

People unwittingly injure even those dear to them, including members of their families. Such thoughtlessness may raise a barrier to friendship and love. The eve of the Day of Atonement is considered an appropriate time to remove these barriers; relatives and friends call upon each other or write, offering good wishes for the coming year and either directly or indirectly asking forgiveness for any misunderstanding. Parents and grandparents bless their children and grandchildren. The moving prayer which is recited just before the evening service closes with the words: "I completely forgive anyone who has committed a trespass against me, whether against my person or against my property. . . . May no man suffer punishment because of me. And may it be Thy will, that just as I offer my forgiveness to all my fellows, that I may find grace in their eyes, so that they, too, will forgive my trespasses against them."

The Day of Atonement thus becomes a day for the renewal of bonds of affection and friendship between men.

The evening service in the synagogue, which must be recited before dark, is called *kol nidre* from its first words (meaning "all vows"). It is a service of absolution for ceremonial vows. This ceremony is made necessary by the rule of Jewish Law, requiring the fulfilment of a vow, even at great sacrifice. The vows which the ceremony of *kol nidre* releases are of course only those relating to ritual and custom. Without the consent of his neighbor, no ceremony can release anyone from a vow or promise made to his neighbor.

Because the *kol nidre* opens the service of the Day of

Atonement, it is a particularly solemn ceremony. Its melody is probably the best known of all those associated with synagogue services.

The Day of Atonement is the major fast in the Jewish calendar, a day on which all principal physical pleasures are interdicted. Men of piety also avoid wearing shoes made of leather on this day, particularly in the home or in the synagogue.[6]

The prayers of *Yom Kippur* day are so arranged that they continue uninterruptedly from their beginning in the morning until their end in the *neilah* service after sunset. At each service, there is a confession of sins and a prayer for forgiveness. During the additional prayer of the morning (*musaf*) there is a reenactment of part of the ancient service at the Temple. In the course of it, the members or at least the elders of the congregation prostrate themselves four times, just as the community gathered in the ancient Temple prostrated itself whenever the Divine Name was pronounced in the service.

The melodies of each of the *Yom Kippur* services follow definite traditions, and are reflective of the mood in which the service is expected to be pronounced. In the course of these services (as well as in those of *Rosh Ha-Shanah*) the Ark is frequently opened for the recital of especially impressive hymns and poems. The service of the Day of Atonement ends with the sounding of the ram's horn, and the joint cry by all of the congregation, "Hear, O Israel, the Lord is our God, the Lord is One."

There is a curious difference between Palestine and other countries with regard to the observance of the Jewish festivals. In Palestine Passover is observed for only

[6] Shoes or sandals were considered an object of luxury in the ancient Orient. It was therefore considered improper to wear them on days of fasting or mourning.

seven days, in accordance with the rule set down in Exodus 12.15; outside Palestine it is observed for eight days. Similarly Pentecost and *Shemini Azeret* are each observed for only one day in Palestine, but for two days outside Palestine. Moreover, in Palestine work is forbidden only on the first and seventh days of Passover, and on the first day of *Sukkot;* outside Palestine it is forbidden also on the second and on the eighth day of Passover, and on the second day of *Sukkot.*

The reason for this variation of custom is historical. In ancient times the beginning of the Jewish month was fixed when the authorities of the Temple in Jerusalem observed the new moon. As the lunar month had been accurately measured in antiquity, it was comparatively easy to foretell when the moon ought to appear in Jerusalem. But the first crescent of the new moon is frequently so thin, and sets so soon after the sun, that it was quite impossible to be certain that it had actually been observed. There was always some doubt therefore by those away from Jerusalem as to whether the Temple authorities had proclaimed one day or the next as the beginning of the calendar month.

To meet this difficulty, Temple authorities would send out messengers informing distant communities of the precise day they had fixed as new moon. These messengers were, of course, able to reach all parts of Palestine in a comparatively short time. They could not reach the distant communities of Babylonia. Hence, the Babylonian Jews were always in doubt as to whether the month had begun on the precise day of the new moon, or the day following. This put them in doubt regarding the exact day of all the festivals. Therefore, in order to avoid any possible violation of a holy day, they observed all the customs relating to each festival for an additional day. In the fifth century of the Christian era, the Jewish calendar was reduced to a fixed computative system, and thereafter no one could be in doubt with regard to the time of a festival. Nevertheless, the Jews outside of Palestine continued to observe their ancient custom. In Palestine, uncertainty regarding the precise period of the festival could occur only with regard to *Rosh Ha-Shanah,* which occurs on the first day of the month. Hence, *Rosh Ha-Shanah* is observed for two days in Palestine as well as in other countries. It is not customary to observe the Day of Atonement for two days, because it is considered impossible to impose the severity of two successive days of fasting on the whole community. Reform Jews have, in general, abandoned the observance of the second day of the holidays.

In addition to these major festivals, whose celebration is commanded in the Law of Moses, there are two lesser festivals in Judaism, which are occasions of great religious joy and sense of communion with God: *Purim,* the Feast of Esther, and *Hanukkah,* the feast signifying the rededication of the Temple during the time of the Maccabees.

In accordance with the prescription of the Book of Esther, *Purim* (occurring in the first half of March) is celebrated as a day of rejoicing and thanksgiving, with the exchange of gifts between friends, and charity to the poor. The Book of Esther is read publicly both at the evening and at the morning services. In the late afternoon, a family festival, second in importance only to that of the *seder* service, is usually held. This festive dinner is called the *seudat purim* (*Purim* meal).

Hanukkah (the midwinter festival which occurs in the

month of December) is celebrated in commemoration of the purification of the Temple by the Maccabees, after it had been defiled by the Syrian King, Antiochus IV, in the year 168 before the Christian era. Led by Judas the Maccabee, the Jews won amazing victories over outnumbering Syrian armies, and finally reconquered Jerusalem, drove the pagans out of the Temple, and reestablished it as a place for the worship of God. The day of the rededication of the Temple was the third anniversary of its first defilement, the twenty-fifth of *Kislev,* and that day, together with seven succeeding days, is observed as *Hanukkah* (the feast of dedication).

On the first night of *Hanukkah* a candle is lit, and on each succeeding night of the eight day festival, an additional candle is lit, in celebration of the holiday. It is also customary to mark the festival with family meals, games, and the exchange of gifts, particularly within the family.

Besides *Yom Kippur,* there are several lesser fasts in the Jewish calendar. Of these the most important is *Tisha B'ab* (popularly pronounced *Tishoh B'ov*), the ninth day of the month of *Ab,* the anniversary of the burning of the first and also of the second Temple. In memory of these catastrophes, it is the rule to fast from sunset on the evening before this day, until the sunset of the day itself. The Book of Lamentations is recited in the evening, and in the morning a number of dirges recording ancient and mediaeval sufferings of the Jewish people. To increase a sense of bereavement it is customary in many communities to spend the afternoon of *Tisha B'ab* visiting the graves of relatives.

There are several other fasts, less commonly observed, during which food is forbidden only during the day. These are the fast of *Gedaliah* (on the day following *Rosh*

Ha-Shanah); the tenth day of the month of *Tebet;* and the seventeenth day of the month of *Tammuz.* All these fasts are mentioned in Zechariah 8.19. The fast of *Gedaliah* commemorates the murder of the last governor of Judah in the year 586 before the Christian era (Jeremiah 41.2). The fast of *Tebet* commemorates the beginning of the siege of Jerusalem by the Babylonians (Ezekiel 24.1-2). The seventeenth day of *Tammuz* is the anniversary of the breach in the wall of Jerusalem by the Romans in the year 70 of the Christian era.

Partial mourning is still observed during the three weeks between the seventeenth day of *Tammuz* and the ninth of *Ab,* the period when Jerusalem was pillaged by the victorious Roman soldiery. No weddings are performed; other festivities and the wearing of new clothes are considered inappropriate. During the last nine days of this period, it is customary for many Jews to abstain from meat and wine (except on the Sabbath day).

The Jewish religious calendar begins in the autumn with *Rosh Ha-Shanah,* the festival of the New Year. The names of the months were adopted from the Babylonian calendar and are as follows: *Tishri, Marchesvan* (frequently called *Heshvan*), *Kislev, Tebet, Shebat, Adar, Nisan, Iyyar, Sivan, Tammuz, Ab, Ellul.*

The length of the month is fixed by the lunar cycle of twenty-nine and a half days and therefore is alternately twenty-nine and thirty days. The length of the year of twelve months is thus 354 days, though under special circumstances it may be 353 or 355 days. To make up the difference between this period and that of the solar year of 365¼ days, an additional month is added to the year, seven times in a cycle of nineteen years. This additional month is added immediately before *Nisan* (the month of the Passover) and is called the Second *Adar*. The additional month is added on the third, the sixth, the eighth, the eleventh, the fourteenth, the seventeenth, and the nineteenth years of the cycle.

Because of the character of the Jewish calendar, the beginning of each month coincides with the new moon, and the first days of the festivals of Passover and *Sukkot* (falling on the fifteenth day of their respective months) occur on the full moon.

VIII. SPECIAL OCCASIONS IN THE COURSE OF LIFE

The occasions of special joy or sadness in human life are, in Judaism, surrounded with ceremonials intended to make them means for closer communion with God. These ceremonials aid the Jew to temper joy with solemnity, and sorrow with resignation. When he is happy, the Jew is instructed to think with gratitude of God, Who is the source of happiness; and when he is in grief, he is likewise instructed to look to God, as the source of consolation. Birth, marriage, and death are thus more than incidents in temporal and sensual existence. They are occasions for thinking more deeply than usual about the meaning of existence, and the relation of man to God.

Every person born of Jewish parents (as indicated above) is considered bound to observe the covenant of Sinai, and therefore subject to the observance of Jewish ceremonial. Although mixed marriages are prohibited, the child of a Jewish mother is regarded as a Jew and needs undergo no ceremony of conversion to be admitted to the Jewish faith. A member of another faith who desires to be converted to Judaism, must (according to traditional ritual) appear before a rabbi and state his desire to be converted. The rabbi will then provide for his instruction in the elements of Jewish law, belief and practice. Before admitting him to the Jewish fold, the rabbi must warn him of the severe discipline of Judaism and the difficulties involved in adherence to the Jewish faith. If the applicant persists in his desire to enter the Jewish faith, the rabbi will arrange for the ceremony of proselytization. A male applicant must be circumcised. According to the traditional ritual followed by orthodox and conservative Jews, both male and female applicants become proselytes by immersion in a pool of running water, declaring that they are performing the ceremony in order to be admitted into the Jewish faith, and reciting as they emerge from the water the benediction, "Blessed art Thou, O Lord, our God, King of the Universe, Who didst sanctify us with Thy commandments, and hast commanded us regarding the ceremonial immersion of the proselyte." Reform rabbis do not include this ritual immersion in their ceremony of proselytization.

In accordance with the prescriptions of Genesis 17.9-14, the son of Jewish parents is circumcised on the eighth day of his life. The ceremony may be postponed for reasons of health. Because the ritual of circumcision involves at once a knowledge of surgery and of the traditional customs, it is performed by a person especially trained for the purpose, called a *mohel* (one who circumcises). At the circumcision, the father recites the benediction, "Blessed art Thou, O Lord, our God, King of the Universe, Who didst consecrate us with Thy commandments, and hast commanded us to bring this child into the covenant of our ancestor, Abraham." All those present respond, "Just as he has entered the covenant of Abraham, may he also enter into the study of the Law, into marriage, and into good deeds!" The *mohel* or some other person present, then prays for the child's future piety and welfare, and announces his name.

A girl is named at the service in the synagogue on the

Sabbath (or any other day when the Torah is read) following her birth, when the father is called to participate in the reading of the Torah. One of those present then prays for the health of the mother of the child, and for the health of the child, and announces its name.

Boys under thirteen years of age and girls under twelve years of age, are theoretically not obligated to observe the discipline of the ritual Law. In order to be trained in the Law, they are expected to observe such parts of it as they can without impairing their health. As soon as a child can speak, he is taught to recite simple evening and morning prayers, consisting primarily of the first verse of the *Shema.* When the child reaches school age, he is taught the Hebrew language, the Bible, and as he grows older, advanced Jewish studies. The instruction is given the child by his parents, by a private teacher, or in a religious school. The traditional school devoted to this purpose is called a *Talmud Torah* (the place of the study of the Law). In America, these institutions usually provide instruction for children for either three or five (in some instances, seven or ten) hours per week, after the regular secular school hours on weekdays, and on Sunday mornings. There are also Jewish day schools established in some communities, providing both secular and religious education. These are sometimes called *yeshibot* (singular, *yeshibah* or *yeshivah,* academy). The name *yeshibah* or *yeshivah* is also used for traditional schools of advanced Talmudic study in Europe, and for similar institutions in America.

A month before a boy has reached his thirteenth birthday, he is expected to begin to don the *tephillin* each morning. On the Sabbath following his thirteenth birthday, he is called to participate in the formal reading of the Torah at the usual synagogue service. The ceremony of which this is part is popularly called *bar mitzvah* (son of the commandment, in reference to his obligation to perform the commandments thereafter). Parents frequently arrange a festive celebration in honor of this occasion.

In many American synagogues similar note is taken when a girl attains the age of twelve, and therefore becomes subject to the commandments. The ceremony which is called *bat mitzvah* (daughter of the commandment, popularly pronounced *bas mitzvah*) is variously observed in different communities. In some of them, the girl is permitted to read the prophetic portion in the vernacular. In others, there is simply a family festivity.

Many conservative and reform congregations have established, either in lieu of these *bar mitzvah* and *bat mitzvah* ceremonies, or in addition to them, that of confirmation. This ritual is usually observed on Pentecost. Boys and girls of the ages of fourteen to sixteen are taught the elements of Jewish faith and history in pre-confirmation classes, and are then called to announce their devotion to the faith at a public synagogue ceremonial.

There is a considerable difference between the marriage customs of traditional and reform Jews. In the traditional service, marriages take place under a canopy (*huppah*), which symbolizes the home established through the marriage.

Judaism regards complete mutual understanding and trust between the bride and the bridegroom as a basic requirement for a valid marriage. A number of ceremonies have been established to give expression to this conception, and there are even several legal forms which emphasize it.

Before the wedding, the rabbi or other person in charge of the ceremony asks the bridegroom whether he undertakes to fulfil all the traditional obligations of a Jewish husband to his wife. These include various traditional provisions for the maintenance of the wife, both during married life, and if the occasion should arise, during her widowhood. As these are civil obligations, a formal agreement must be made to provide for them. On the bridegroom's assenting, the ceremony of *kinyan* (agreement) is performed. This consists of the rabbi handing the bridegroom an object of value, usually a handkerchief, as a symbolic consideration, to make the bridegroom's acceptance of the conditions of the marriage valid. The rabbi then draws up a document called a *ketubah* (writ, popularly pronounced *kesubah*) detailing these obligations as well as those of the wife. This *ketubah* is witnessed by two observant Jews, neither of whom may be related to the bride or bridegroom. The officiating rabbi may also act as one of these witnesses.

The language of the *ketubah* is Aramaic, the vernacular of the Jews of Palestine during the period when the present text was composed. The document is sometimes artistically decorated; and a number of the *ketubot* preserved in various museums of Jewish antiquities are of great interest to the student of art.

The wedding ceremony itself consists of a series of benedictions, having for their purpose the expression of thanks to God for the institution of marriage and the family, for having implanted His image on the human race, and for the joy of the wedding, and including prayers for the happiness of the bride and bridegroom, and for the restoration of Jerusalem. After the first of these benedictions, the bridegroom hands the bride a ring, and says to her in Hebrew, "Thou art sanctified unto me, with this ring, in accordance with the Law of Moses and of Israel." At the end of the ceremony a glass is broken, to commemorate the destruction of Jerusalem.

In the marriage service of the reform group, the canopy and the *ketubah* are generally omitted. The wedding is usually celebrated in the synagogue. The special prayer for the restoration of Jerusalem is omitted. On the other hand, several prayers, in English, on behalf of the bride and the bridegroom, are added. The service ends with the recitation of the priestly blessing (Numbers 6.24-26) by the rabbi.[7]

Jewish Law forbids husband and wife to cohabit or to come into physical contact during the period of menstruation or for seven days afterward. At the end of the period, the wife is required to take a ritual bath in a pool of running water, or one especially built for the purpose (*mikveh*). A bride also bathes in such a *mikveh* before her wedding. The value of these regulations in preserving Jewish family life and in the prevention of certain diseases, has been recognized by various Christian and Jewish writers on genetics.[8]

In Jewish Law marriage can be terminated by a religious divorce (called *get*). In practice such a divorce is granted by a rabbi only if both parties consent, and have already been divorced in the civil courts. The ritual of divorce is extremely complicated, and is performed only by especially trained scholars. Reform rabbis generally recognize a civil divorce as terminating a Jewish marriage, from a religious as well as from the secular point of view,

[7] *Rabbi's Manual,* edited and published by the Central Conference of American Rabbis, Cincinnati, 1928, p. 39, ff.

[8] For a further discussion and bibliography, see Mrs. R. L. Jung, in *The Jewish Library,* edited by Rabbi Leo Jung, Third Series, pp. 355-365.

and therefore do not insist on a religious divorce as prerequisite for remarriage of either husband or wife.

There is one instance in traditional Jewish Law in which the death of the husband does not completely break the marriage bond; that is the case of a childless widow, described in Deuteronomy 25.5-10. Biblical Law, as stated in Deuteronomy, requires such a childless widow to marry her husband's brother, so that her first-born son, by the second marriage, may "succeed in the name of the brother which is dead, that his name be not put out of Israel." Later rabbinic ordinances forbade the performance of such a Levirate marriage, but nevertheless insisted that the widow may not remarry without performing the ceremony of *halitzah,* ordained in Deuteronomy, as alternative to such a marriage.

When a Jew feels that his end is approaching, he should confess his sins in accordance with the fixed ritual, making special mention, however, of any sin which he is conscious of having committed, and which is not mentioned in the traditional formula. In his last conscious moments, he recites the traditional confession of faith, "Hear, O Israel, the Lord is our God, the Lord is One." Those about him may help him recite the formula, by repeating it with him.

According to rabbinic tradition, the body should be washed after death and dressed in linen shrouds. The universal use of linen shrouds dates back to the beginning of the second century of the Christian era. Rabban Gamaliel II, the head of the Academy of Jabneh and one of the most distinguished scholars and communal leaders of his time, specifically requested that no elaborate provision such as was then customary be made for his burial, but that he be interred in a shroud like those used for the poor. The custom has been universally adopted by observant Jews to stress further the equality of all men.

The body must be interred in the ground, as soon after death as possible. Cremation is forbidden, as being an implicit denial of the resurrection.

The funeral service is usually recited in the home of the deceased, though in the case of a person of especial piety, it may be recited in the synagogue. Because of the conditions of modern urban life, funeral services are sometimes held in rooms especially devoted to that purpose, so-called funeral chapels. The purpose of the service and the ceremonies associated with it, is to give expression to the natural grief of the bereaved, and at the same time to inculcate in the bereaved resignation to the will of God.

The service consists of the recital of one or more psalms and selections of appropriate verses from other psalms. Usually Psalm 16, 23, 90, or 91 is recited. The reading of the psalm may be followed by an address; and the service closes with a prayer for the peace of the soul of the deceased. This prayer is repeated at the grave, and a second psalm is recited, after which the bereaved recite the *kaddish*. Either during the funeral services or immediately before the burial, the person officiating at the ceremonies asks the near relatives of the deceased (husband, wife, son, daughter, father, mother, brother, or sister) to cut one of their garments. This ceremony is called *keriah* (tearing the garment) and is reminiscent of the ancient Jewish usage of tearing one's clothes in bereavement (see II Samuel 1.11). After tearing the garment, each of the bereaved recites the blessing of resignation to the justice of God: "Blessed art Thou, O Lord, our God, King of the Universe, the true Judge."

During the week after the burial of a relative, near

relatives, including husband, wife, children, brothers, sisters, and parents, remain at home. They must not engage in any gainful occupation, unless the income is vital to their subsistence, or unless they will forfeit their employment. It is customary for friends to visit the mourners to console them, and to arrange public prayers in the house of the deceased. During the whole week of mourning (called *shiva,* seven, i.e., the seven days of mourning) a lamp is kept burning in the house of the deceased. None of the mourners wears any jewels, and mirrors, considered a luxury, are covered. The mourners sit on low stools, instead of chairs; they do not study the Law or the Scriptures, save such solemn works as the Books of Job and Lamentations, the dire prophecies in Jeremiah, and the laws of mourning in the Talmud and Codes; and they are forbidden to wear shoes made of leather.

After the completion of the *shiva,* the relatives observe partial mourning for the remainder of the month. They do not don new clothes, and avoid taking part in festivities, or listening to music. On the death of a parent, this partial mourning is observed for a whole year. In order to make grief itself a means for closer communion with God, the child is expected, during this year of mourning, to be particularly mindful of religious observances, to attend synagogue service regularly, and to recite the *kaddish* at each prayer. Whenever possible, the bereaved son serves as reader of the public prayers on weekdays during this year of mourning. These customs are also observed on the anniversary of the death of one's parents. Such an anniversary is called *yahrzeit* (a German name, because the custom assumed its present form among the German Jews). It is customary, also, to have a light burning at home during the day marking the anniversary of the death of a near relative. This light symbolizes the belief in human immortality, in accordance with the rabbinic interpretation of the verse (Proverbs 20.27), "The spirit of man is the lamp of God, searching all the inward parts." About a year after the death of a relative, the mourners set up a monument marking the place of the grave. At the unveiling of this monument, called *maṣṣebah* (pillar, popularly pronounced *matzevah*), psalms are read, prayers are recited for the peace of the soul of the deceased, and the *kaddish* is repeated.

IX. THE JEWISH HOME AND THE DIETARY LAWS

Like every other authentic experience, training, or ambition, piety cannot stop short of the home. If religion were to be merely ecclesiastical, it would soon cease to be that, too. The psalmist who was told "Let us go up to the house of the Lord," rejoiced because in his own house the reality of God was never forgotten. Throughout Jewish history indeed the attempt to reproduce in the home the order and mood of the place of worship has never been relaxed.

The interrelationship of sanctuary and home has been responsible for at least two significant results. On the one hand, the Jew did not remain a stranger to the ceremonial and purpose of his sacred institutions. On the other hand, his home and home life were transfigured. His residence became a habitation of God. What might have been nothing more than a functional shelter acquired a surplus value.

This sanctification of the home was achieved by a religious discipline whose purpose was constantly to prompt a remembrance of God. The Jew who visited the ancient Temple, for example, readily understood that the elaborate rites, precautions, exactitudes, purifications, were the appropriate expressions of the beauty of holiness. "If you were to serve a king of flesh and blood," the saintly Hillel once reminded a guest, "would you not have to learn how to make your entrances and exits and obeisances?

How much more so in the service of the King of kings of kings!"

That such fastidiousness was therefore required in God's House the Jew accepted as unquestioningly as we accept beautiful form on occasions of state or solemnity. The forms reminded him of God. And because they did, and because Israel's teachers tried to prevent the Jew from forgetting God even when he was away from the Sanctuary, corresponding rituals and attitudes were introduced into the Jewish home. Thus the Jewish home became a sanctuary in miniature, its table an altar, its furnishings instruments for sanctity.

In a sense, every detail of home life is an expression of the pattern of sanctity. Jewish homes, for example, are generally expected to contain the basic religious texts like the Bible, usually accompanied at least with the commentary of Rashi, the Talmud, perhaps an abbreviated code (the short Shulhan Aruk), some of the magnificent moralistic works, and of course the Prayer Book—which is actually one of the most extraordinary anthologies of Jewish classical literature. It is not uncommon to find in a traditional Jewish home an excellent library with volumes which have been handed down from father to son, volumes which reveal constant use. Just as we might say that no cultured home lacks its Shakespeare volumes, its classics, its pictures, so the Jew would say that no home, since it is a field for holiness, can be fully furnished without the literature which teaches man about God.

Similarly, the various family festival celebrations with their rituals (see above chapter VII) constitute activities which bring the divine message very close to the Jew. It is an insensitive Jewish child indeed who forgets the beauty of the Seder at Passover, or the kindling of the lights during Hanukkah, or the sight of his mother kindling the Sabbath lamps at dusk. These and like activities collaborate to make holiness a familiar emphasis and delight.

Part of the daily pattern of sanctity is formed by the so called dietary laws. As is well known, Jewish law prohibits the eating of certain foods. These prohibitions are enumerated essentially in Leviticus, chapter 11, and again in Deuteronomy, chapter 14. No vegetable growths are prohibited; but of animal life the Law permits fish which have scales and fins, certain types of fowl, and only those quadrupeds which chew their cud and have cloven hoofs. Among the domestic quadrupeds this includes only oxen, sheep, and goats.

According to traditional Judaism, warm blooded animals may be eaten only if they are ritually slaughtered, i.e., if they are slaughtered in the manner used in the Temple for sacrificial purposes. The knife used in slaughtering must be sharp, and must be examined both before and after slaughtering, to be certain that its edge contains no notch, which by tearing the animal's throat might give it unnecessary pain. The animal must not, however, be stunned before slaughtering, for stunning prevents the free flow of the blood, and the absorption of the blood in the meat makes the food prohibited. To insure the animal's speedy death, the person who slays it must be trained for the work. He must be capable of examining the knife to be sure that it contains no notch; he must know enough of the diseases of animals to be able to examine the body, and to make certain that it was suffering from no serious disease. A person so trained is called a *shohet* (slaughterer). In order to be allowed to perform his duties, he must receive authorization from a rabbi.

After an animal is slaughtered, its lungs are examined to guard against symptoms of various communicable diseases, mainly tuberculosis. The Talmud, its commentaries, and the later codes, contain an impressive amount of veterinary information regarding the symptoms of disease in animals, so that an examination based on this information is a means of detecting disease.

If an animal has been found to be free from serious disease, its meat is declared *kasher* (fit, popularly pronounced *kosher*).

The meat must not, however, remain unwashed for three days. If it does, the surface blood is believed to be absorbed in the tissues; and the food becomes prohibited. After the meat is cut, the various parts are placed in a container of water for half an hour to be cleansed of such surface blood as adheres to them. Thereafter the meat is covered with salt, further to draw out the blood, and remains in the salt for at least an hour. The salt is then washed off, and the meat may be boiled. Meat which is to be roasted on a spit need not be soaked in water or salted. Meat from the udder or the liver may be prepared only by roasting.

In addition to the various laws prohibiting certain types of food, there is a rule mentioned thrice in the Scripture against seething a kid in its mother's milk (Exodus 23.19; 34.26; and Deuteronomy 14.21). This rule was originally intended, according to Maimonides, to extirpate an idolatrous practice. It is interpreted as prohibiting the cooking or eating the meat of any warm blooded animal with milk, or a derivative of milk. Hence, it is prohibited to serve meat and milk or butter or cheese at the same meal. In order to avoid any possibility of a mixture of meat and milk, observant Jews provide themselves with two types of dishes, one of which is used only for meat foods, the other only for milk foods. Further, it is customary in many countries not to eat milk dishes for six hours after a meat meal.

Scripture is quite brief in outlining the regulations governing diet, so that the various theories about the dietary laws remain in the last analysis purely speculative. Why certain animals should have been permitted and why others should have been forbidden as food we do not know. But the purpose for these regulations is explicitly stated (see Leviticus 11:45): "Be ye therefore holy, for I (the Lord) am holy."

X. THE JEWISH HOPE FOR THE FUTURE

Virtually every prophet in Scripture has predicted that in the fulness of time, man will gain a more complete understanding of God, and will inaugurate a reign of justice and peace on earth. According to the interpretation of this prophecy in the Talmud and later writers, this age of universal peace will be established by a great, but humble teacher of the lineage of David: the Messiah. Reform and many conservative Jews, on the other hand, expect that the Messianic age will come about through the gradual enlightenment of men, and through the work of many thinkers and teachers. All agree that the age will be one of profound and universal faith in God, recognition of human brotherhood, and an unprecedented knowledge of the universe. There will be no discrimination between persons because of sex, origin, faith, occupation, nationality, or any other reason. The evils of human origin will have been overcome; those inherent in Nature will be mitigated through further knowledge and increased piety. In this world of brotherly love, there will be no room for pride in achievement, nor for memories of past bitterness and oppression.

The prophetic tradition, originating in the teachings of Moses, may be considered a continuous endeavor, looking to the fulfilment of this vision. Together with other faiths derived from Scripture, Judaism has a unique contribution to make to the enlightenment of the world. Its special contribution consists, in part, in the preservation of the Hebrew language, and the original form of the Hebrew Scriptures, as well as in the transmission unchanged of the ethical, ceremonial, and intellectual discipline which were native to the Prophets and the later sages.

The increase of hatred and persecution in our day does not weaken the Jew's faith in God and in His prophets or his conviction that ultimately the age of universal human brotherhood will be established on earth. In the most trying moments of his own and world history, the Jew repeats, with assurance, the ancient declaration, "Thou art faithful, O Lord, our God, and Thy words are faithful. And not one word of Thine shall ultimately remain unfulfilled; for Thou art a great, holy, Divine King."

INDEX

INDEX

INDEX

INDEX

PART II

THE ROMAN CATHOLIC RELIGION IN CREED AND LIFE

BY J. ELLIOT ROSS

BIBLIOGRAPHY

The Catholic Encyclopedia.

Codex Juris Canonici, 1917.

Outline History of the Catholic Church, by Rev. Joseph McSorley.

"Certain Difficulties Felt by Anglicans in Catholic Teaching Considered," vol. II, *Cardinal Newman.*

Moral Theology, Callan & McHugh, 1929.

Essay on the Development of Doctrine, by John Henry Newman.

The Question Box, Bertrand Conway.

The Manual of Prayers.

A Doctrine of Hope, by Bishop Boromelli.

The New Catholic Dictionary.

The Imitation of Christ, by Thomas à Kempis,

Introduction to a Devout Life, St. Francis de Sales.

Practice of the Presence of God, Brother Lawrence.

Heliotropium, Drexelius.

The Spiritual Exercises, St. Ignatius.

Sancta Sophia, Francis Baker.

The Mansions of the Soul, St. Teresa of Avila.

Dark Night of the Soul, St. John of the Cross.

Encyclical of Leo XIII, "Libertas, Praestantissimum."

The Church and War, Franziskus Stratman, N. Y., 1928.

The Church and Society, Dr. F. Ernest Johnson, N. Y., 1935.

Commentaries on the Constitution of the United States, Justice Story.

I. INTRODUCTION

1. The Distinguishing Characteristic of Roman Catholicism

THE Roman Catholic Church, according to the definition of the Baltimore Catechism, "is the congregation of all those who profess the faith of Christ, partake of the same Sacraments, and are governed by their lawful pastors under one visible Head." Then it goes on to say that "the Pope, the Bishop of Rome, is the visible Head of the Church."

Since the Bishop of Rome is called "Pope," etymologically the words "Popery," "Papist," "Romanism," and such like might seem to be applicable. But Roman Catholics do not like these terms because at one time or another they have been used in a derogatory sense. Throughout this essay the "Roman" will be dropped for the sake of convenience, and merely the terms "Catholic," "Catholicism," the "Church" will be used.[1]

Belief in the Pope's authority marks off Catholicism from all other religions. For this reason it seems best to begin with an explanation of papal authority, rather than

[1] To furnish a fairly complete idea of Catholicism would require several large volumes. The attempt is here made only to give for those who are not Catholics an understandable sketch of Catholic belief and practice. Those interested in knowing more on particular phases will find a completer treatment in the books to which from time to time reference is made. *The Catholic Encyclopedia,* available in many public libraries, covers the field in fifteen quarto volumes. An index volume facilitates the finding of any topic not accorded a separate article.

with the broader question of the authority of the Church. According to Catholic belief, papal authority is based on the will of Christ in establishing His Church. God, we believe, chose this way.

The Pope's *religious* authority—which is the only authority the Pope has over Catholics in the United States—is divided into *teaching* authority and *governing* authority. Both are intended for the Church universally, and so are concerned only with matters having a broad application. The Pope does not attempt, and has no authority, to regulate the minute personal life of an individual Catholic. He never says to an individual, for instance, speaking as Pope: "You enter such-and-such a seminary next September," or "You, John Jones, will be following God's will for you individually if you marry Elizabeth Smith in June."

Further, the teaching authority of the Pope may be subdivided into fallible and infallible authority. Not every declaration of the Pope is infallible. But all papal pronouncements, even those recognized as fallible, must be received respectfully.

Papal infallibility means that when certain conditions are fulfilled what the Pope teaches is true and binding upon the intellect of the faithful. Those who wish to remain in communion with the Catholic Church must accept such infallible papal teaching.

The conditions necessary for the exercise of this infallible or *ex cathedra* teaching authority are these:

1) The Pope must speak as the Supreme Head of the Church, and not simply as a private theologian, or as a cardinal.

2) He must address the whole Church and not merely a part of it, as the Church in Germany or in America; be-

cause his prerogative of infallibility is for the Church Universal.

3) He must speak on a question of faith or morals

4) That has been revealed in *Scripture* or in *Tradition*. These two italicized words will be more fully explained later.

5) And, finally, he must make clear his intention of using his infallible teaching authority.

From this it is evident that not everything the Pope says must be considered by Catholics as infallibly true. He does not have to use his infallible teaching authority, and does not do so in all his utterances. Hence it may happen that there is a discrepancy between some statements of different Popes, just as there may be a discrepancy between some statements of two theologians. Furthermore, the Pope's infallible authority does not extend to secular subjects. Since it is restricted to what has been revealed in Scripture or in Tradition it has no power of new revelation. Infallibility is not inspiration such as the authors of Scripture enjoyed, but rather a protection from error in interpreting what inspired authors have uttered.

Because infallibility is thus restricted to the interpretation of what has been revealed, it has no application to the governing authority of the Pope. He may make mistakes in governing, and some of his laws may be inadvisable. A perfectly loyal Catholic may think that some ecclesiastical legislation is out of date and should be changed. Papal governing authority touches the will, not the intellect, of the subjects. As a matter of fact, the Popes themselves have shown that their legislation needed changing from time to time by actually changing it.

Still less does infallibility imply impeccability. Even the best popes have their human frailties and go to confession

—some daily. In the long history of the Church a few decidedly wicked men have secured election to the office of Pope and disgraced it by their deeds. But the private life of a Pope, no matter how sinful, does not prevent a Pope from infallibly interpreting God's Revelation. And because infallible papal utterances are rare events, it might easily happen that whatever such there were would be made only by reasonably good Popes. Infallibility and the personal morality of a Pope are two distinct things.

The infallibility of the Pope is a personal prerogative and cannot be transferred to a subordinate. But papal infallibility is never exercised in a completely autocratic manner. The Pope always takes into consideration the opinion of theologians on a particular point before issuing his decision. Indeed, most questions decided by the ultimate infallible teaching authority of the Pope have previously been discussed for centuries. The Church is slow to give her final infallible decision, although that authority is always there if an appeal to it becomes necessary as the only way of settling some controversy.

Papal authority, Catholics believe, is part of the divine authority of the Church. This divine authority may be exercised through a General Council—an assembly of the bishops of the world called by the Pope—, the teaching of theologians, the general belief of the Church (*Ecclesia credens*), as well as by papal pronouncements. Hence propositions proposed for the belief of Catholics may be drawn from different founts, and have different theological notes attached to them.

For instance, some propositions are called "Of Faith" (*De Fide*) and must be believed by all Catholics. Then, in a diminishing scale of strictness of the obligation to believe, come propositions which are "certain," "common opinions," and "more common opinions."

Attached to the denial of any proposition is a note of censure corresponding to the degree of authority possessed by the proposition. Thus one who denies what is "Of Faith" is a heretic. But if a proposition is only "certain" its contradiction is "rash." [1] The denial of a "common opinion" is called "offensive to pious ears." A "more common opinion" naturally implies that there is a "less common opinion." Some Catholics believe what other Catholics do not believe. It is at least "certain" that the phrase "outside the Church there is no salvation" is not to be interpreted as requiring membership in the visible organization of the Church for salvation. But if one took the opposite view he would not be, strictly speaking, a heretic.

Of course, the ordinary lay Catholic knows nothing of these theological technicalities in regard to the authority of various propositions. And yet he does have some idea of a sphere in which Catholics may differ. Possibly he has read books with an "imprimatur," [2] maybe from the same bishop, which take opposite views on a particular point; or he may have heard sermons by different priests expressing contradictory views. Not being themselves infallible, Catholics may at times accuse someone of heresy who is simply exercising his freedom of belief in a sphere where it is allowed.

By his governing authority the Pope makes laws to regulate the conduct of Catholics generally.[3] Because these

[1] "If all theologians teach as true or (aut) certain a doctrine which of itself belongs to faith or morals, it is rash to reject it." (Synopsis Theol. Dogmat. A. Tanquerey, ed. 23, vol. I, par. 979.)

[2] The *Nihil Obstat* and *Imprimatur* appearing in a Catholic book simply mean that in the opinion of the Ordinary granting the *Imprimatur* the book contains nothing contrary to the teaching of the Church. They do not mean that a Catholic must believe every statement contained in the book.

[3] The *Codex Juris Canonici* issued in 1917 contains these laws. But Canon Law, just as does Civil Law, requires technical training for its understanding. Hence there are numerous commentaries on the Code. A

ecclesiastical laws are for the Church generally, the Church sometimes grants a dispensation from a particular law.

Also, there are certain recognized principles for the interpretation of canon law which prevent it from working an undue and unintended hardship in individual cases. Probably the most striking of these principles is *"epikia,"* a prudent judgment that if the legislator knew the particular circumstances of a certain individual he would not want the law to apply to that individual. Then there is the principle that a doubtful law does not bind. The agent is assumed to be free unless it is certain that there is legislation to the contrary. Again, a law establishing an obligation is to be interpreted as narrowly as possible, as bringing under it as few subjects and cases as is consistent with a strict construction of its wording; but a law granting a favor is to be interpreted as broadly as its wording allows, bringing under it as many cases and subjects as is consistent with its terms.

Finally, if the inconvenience imposed upon a person by keeping a particular law, as the distance to be traveled in attending Mass on Sunday, is proportionate to the importance of the law, the individual is excused from obeying the law.[1]

Congregation exists in Rome for the official interpretation of the Code when there is a difference of opinion between canonists.

[1] The documents issued by the Pope bear different names according to their character. A papal "Bull" is a major letter, especially the document used in appointing a bishop; whereas a papal "Brief" is a compendious papal letter lacking some of the formality and solemnity of a "Bull." The term "Decree" is principally used of legislative enactments, though it is also used in a wider sense. *"Motu Proprio"* designates an informal method the Pope uses to make a "Decree." "Rescript," the simplest of the papal documents, means a written answer by the Pope. An "Encyclical" is a letter addressed by the Pope to the bishops generally. For these and other terms consult the *Catholic Encyclopedia.*

2. The Organization of the Church

Because the Pope is only one man over 375,000,000 subjects his teaching authority short of infallibility and his governing authority must be shared by others. In Rome are bureaus or departments, called Congregations, assisting the Pope in his work as Head of the Church. Each is made up of cardinals and other ecclesiastics of recognized theological learning. To the appropriate Congregations are referred questions of teaching, or of the meaning of existing legislation, or the advisability of new legislation, as they occur. The decision of the Congregation is approved by the Pope, sometimes in an ordinary, sometimes in a solemn, way.

The decision of a Congregation, unless the Pope makes it his own in an *ex cathedra* statement, is not infallible. And yet from a disciplinary standpoint it may be final. A Congregation's action corresponds somewhat to a decision of the Supreme Court. No one considers the Supreme Court infallible, and yet its decisions must be accepted respectfully and acted upon. Just as the Supreme Court may later practically reverse a previous decision, so, as in the Galileo case, the decision of a Roman Congregation may be practically changed as new light is thrown on a particular problem.

Throughout the world are the bishops. Those in charge of sees are called Ordinaries, and for their see they have a limited teaching and governing authority subject to review by a Roman Congregation and ultimately by the Pope. The Catholic Church is episcopal as well as papal. Each bishop, we believe, has apostolic succession, tracing his authority back through an unbroken succession to the Apostles appointed by Christ Himself. Some bishops who are not Ordinaries have only titular sees. That is, the see from which they take their title—for instance, Bishop of Gadara, now Um Keiss, Palestine—and in which they do not live, long ago ceased to have enough Catholics to warrant an organized hierarchy. All bishops are appointed by the Pope.

A cardinal, as such, has no territorial authority. In itself, the title is honorary, and the recipient may be a simple priest (as was John Henry Newman) or even a layman who is never ordained. Thus Cardinal Antonelli, who was Secretary of State to Pope Pius IX, was not a priest. However, attached to the office of cardinal is the right to vote for the successor of a deceased Pope.[1]

An archbishop, if not merely titular, is Ordinary of an archdiocese. Such an Ordinary has the authority of a bishop over the arch-diocese and some authority over the province composed of the suffragan sees. Generally speaking, however, each bishop is head of his own diocese, directly responsible to the Pope, to whom he must report personally (or in extraordinary cases, by delegate) on his visit *ad limina Apostolorum* (to the thresholds of the Apostles) every three to ten years.

Sometimes Ordinaries have subordinate bishops to assist them in the work of their dioceses. An auxiliary bishop has

[1] For some years the College of Cardinals has been fixed at an upper limit of seventy, but usually there are some vacancies. In the very early times of the Church the people and clergy of Rome elected the Bishop of Rome. Some temporal sovereigns have claimed the right to veto any particular selection of the cardinals for Pope. The last time this veto was exercised was in the conclave to elect a successor to Leo XIII, when the Austrian Emperor opposed Cardinal Rampolla and the conclave chose Cardinal Sarto. He took the name of Pius X and one of his first papal acts was to annul the veto power. There have been a number of antipopes, that is, men who claimed, though not rightly, to have been elected Bishop of Rome. Once there were three such claimants. All this is part of the history of Catholicism, and is too long a story to go into here. A good short history of the Church is that by Rev. Joseph McSorley, *"Outline History of the Catholic Church."*

no right to succeed automatically to the see on the death of the Ordinary; whereas a coadjutor bishop succeeds to the see automatically when the Ordinary dies. Monsignor is a title of honor without any special teaching or governing authority.

An apostolic delegate is the representative of the Pope for ecclesiastical affairs in a particular country. A nuncio is the diplomatic representative of the Pope as a temporal sovereign. A legate is the Pope's representative for some specific work, as presiding at a Eucharistic Congress.

The title of the Pope is "His Holiness," or "Holy Father," of a cardinal "His Eminence." Bishops are called "Most Reverend," monsignors are "Right Reverend" or "Very Reverend," according to their rank.

Each diocese is divided into parishes with geographical limits. However, cutting across the geographical boundaries of the regular parishes, there may be special parishes for those of a particular race or language, as German, Spanish, colored, etc. Over each parish is a pastor appointed by the Ordinary. Some pastors may be removed at the discretion of the Ordinary, but others may be removed only after a canonical trial. Under a pastor there may be, according to the size of the parish, any number of assistant priests. The pastor by the fact of his office has certain rights and duties in regard to the administration of the Sacraments to lay Catholics living in his parish.

Every priest must belong to some diocese or to a religious community. Only with the consent of his own Ordinary (if he is a diocesan priest) and that of the Ordinary of the diocese to which he intends to move may a priest change his diocesan incardination, as it is called. The diocese in which a priest is incardinated has certain obligations in regard to his support.

Although the Catholic Church is an episcopal organization, there are religious communities of various sorts—as Benedictines, Franciscans, Dominicans, Passionists, Jesuits —to which priests may belong instead of to a diocese. Depending upon the constitution of each community, such priests may be sent from one diocese to another independently of the Ordinaries. But to be pastor such a priest needs the approval of the Ordinary in whose diocese is the parish. Some religious communities are technically "exempt" from episcopal jurisdiction in certain regards.

"Once a priest always a priest," means having in perpetuity certain obligations and powers of priesthood. But the proper ecclesiastical authority may for a sufficient reason forbid to a particular priest the exercise of these powers—"suspend" him.

In the Latin rite of the Roman Catholic Church—the rite to which the great majority of priests in the United States belong—priests are celibates. However, a number of rites of the Roman Catholic Church allow a married man to be ordained, but forbid a new marriage to a widower priest. Pope Clement IV was a widower with two daughters when he was elected Pope.

In addition to the clergy, there are communities of Brothers and of Sisters which do much of the Church's work. Most religious communities take the three vows of poverty, chastity, and obedience. However, the members of some religious institutions live in community without taking these vows.

Many religious communities have some special external work, such as teaching or nursing, but some are devoted to a life of contemplation. One may obtain a dispensation from the vows taken as the member of a religious community. A priest religious obtaining a dispensation from his vows of poverty and obedience would become incardinated in some diocese, a Brother or a Sister would return to lay life.

Members of religious communities are often referred to by the term "religious" used as a noun. Priests who are not members of religious communities are called "diocesan" or "secular" priests; members of religious communities, especially those with solemn vows, are often called "the regular clergy."

The Pope has no civil or temporal authority over Catholics in the United States. It is true that the Pope is a temporal sovereign, but his temporal authority is restricted to Vatican City which has a few acres and a few hundred subjects. Still less have bishops or pastors any temporal authority over Catholics.

3. The Place of Conscience in Catholicism

As has been said, the authority of the Pope distinguishes Catholicism from every other religion. Nevertheless, the final authority for the individual may be said to be his "conscience." By "conscience" is here understood a man's practical reason telling him here and now that he is bound by God's moral law to believe or not to believe, to do or not to do, some specific thing. Thus an individual Catholic who is intellectually convinced that he or someone else has had a private revelation is bound conscientiously to believe that revelation. And though as a general thing the conscience of the individual Catholic will tell him that the Pope is right, *if* an individual were convinced that he should not do what the Pope commands, theologians say that the individual would be bound to follow his conscience.

For one who has the use of reason the only way to attain salvation is by living up to one's conscience. And the Catholic position is that anyone believing in God and supernatural sanctions who lives up to his conscience will be saved; whereas anyone who without repentance dies after having seriously transgressed his conscience will be lost.

In his "Letter to the Duke of Norfolk," [1] Cardinal Newman quotes the example given by the Jesuit theologian Busenbaum, that a man brought up to believe the Catholic religion false and that he should do all in his power to oppose it should, *so long as that is his conscience,* follow its dictates. It may be added that no one should become a Catholic except on the conscientious conviction that it is the true religion, and no priest could lawfully receive a convert on any other basis.

The supreme rule for Catholics, then—as, indeed, for everyone—is to obey one's conscience, no matter what that conscience is. Conscience can never be completely surrendered. No external authority can ever be so intimate and omnipresent that it can answer all the innumerable moral problems presented to the individual. Cardinal Newman ends the chapter referred to above: "Certainly, if I am obliged to bring religion into after-dinner toasts (which, indeed, does not seem to me quite the thing), I shall drink—to the Pope, if you please, still to conscience first, and to the Pope afterwards."

Naturally, one has the obligation of informing one's self on moral questions so that one will have a right conscience. Catholics have the same Decalogue as have Jews

[1] Really a book of nearly 300 pages. In Newman's collected works it is in the second volume of *"Certain Difficulties Felt by Anglicans in Catholic Teaching Considered."* Those interested in the authority of conscience in the Catholic religion will find Newman's exposition in 30 pages enlightening and fascinating.

and Protestants. But though all moral questions can be brought under one or other of the Ten Commandments, there is often need of study to see the application. Ability of the reason to make the correct moral decisions is like any other mental ability in that it can be improved or to a large extent lost. The surest way of increasing the keenness of one's conscience is faithfully to follow it where it is clear; and the surest way to dull one's conscience is to disregard its clear dictates.[1]

4. Catholicism and the Bible

Although the human mind by the light of reason can arrive at certain religious truths, such as the existence of God, there are other religious truths which by itself it cannot reach. And for ease and certainty in knowing any religious truths the generality of mankind needs the assistance of God's Revelation. In a strict sense, Revelation is a supernatural imparting by God of truths which man could not know simply by his unaided natural reason; in a broader sense Revelation is any truth made known supernaturally by God; in a still broader sense it is the making known of religious truth even by natural means—"the heavens show forth the glory of God." (Psalms XVIII. 1)

God's Revelation in the strict sense is contained principally in the canonical books of the Bible. For the Old Testament, Catholics accept Wisdom, Ecclesiasticus, Baruch, First and Second Machabees as part of the canonical scriptures. Also, following the Septuagint (the translation of the Old Testament into Greek between 300 and 130 B.C.), Catholics include some passages in Esther and

[1] There are innumerable Catholic treatises covering the whole field of morality. A good one in English is *Moral Theology,* by Callan and McHugh.

Daniel rejected by large bodies of Protestants. Those who hold that these writings are not inspired call them "apocryphal." Catholics restrict the term "apocryphal" to other writings, as the Prayer of Manasses, about whose inspiration there was at one time some doubt, but which were finally rejected by all.

The books of the Old Testament accepted as canonical by both Protestants and Catholics are sometimes named differently by the respective groups. Thus what Protestants call I and II Samuel, Catholics call I and II Kings, while the Protestant I and II Kings are for Catholics III and IV Kings. Proper names in the Catholic version are sometimes transliterated differently by Catholics from the spelling used by Protestants. For example, what Protestants call Ezra, we call Esdras.

The numbering of the Psalms in Protestant and Catholic versions differs, because Protestants divide Psalm X into two Psalms, making Psalm X and Psalm XI. Our Psalm XI is therefore Psalm XII for Protestants, and so on. But the same Psalms (though numbered differently) are accepted by Catholics and Protestants as inspired, and both reject Psalm 151. Again, the numbering of the Ten Commandments differs between Catholics and Protestants, but both have the same Commandments.

The average man, of course, is not capable of deciding between the claims of various books or portions of books to a place in the Bible. Catholics confronted by the massive fact of the Church and believing that the Church was established by Christ with authority to teach, accept from the Church a decision as to what writings are inspired and therefore part of the Bible. After long years of controversy in regard to particular books, the Council of Trent finally decided the canon of the Old and of the New

Testaments for Catholics, and put both sections of the Bible on the same basis. Both are equally the Word of God. And as the Word of God they contain no error.

By saying that the Bible is inspired, Catholics mean that God moved the will and enlightened the intellect of the various writers in such a way that He can be truly called the Author of what they wrote; that they wrote what He intended should be written for the instruction of His Church, and wrote only what God wanted them to write.

However, this does not mean a mechanical or verbal inspiration. God did not dictate the Scriptures to the human authors as if they were stenographers. Nor were they necessarily in a trance as the effect of inspiration. In fact, they could be truly inspired as to their writing without knowing that they were inspired.

Nor does inspiration rule out any particular kind of writing. Poetry, prose, history, fiction may be inspired. Similarly, an inspired writer may quote from an uninspired book, or he may edit uninspired documents. But by the fact of his making them his own they become part of the inspired Scriptures.

Tradition, in its technical sense, is also part of Revelation. Before the first book of the New Testament was written naturally there was no New Testament. But there was a teaching of the Apostles, and Catholics believe that this apostolic teaching was Revelation. Within a generation or two much of this teaching of the Apostles was written down by inspired authors and became part of the canonical Scriptures. But some of the apostolic teaching, though written down by others, was not written by inspired authors and did not become a part of Scripture.

This teaching of the Apostles which is not a part of the Scriptures is "Tradition," and it forms a source of Catholic belief. Catholics, therefore, do not feel compelled to prove every point of doctrine with a text from Scripture. If a particular doctrine is found in Tradition (in this restricted sense of the word) but not in the Bible, yet it is to be believed.

As far as what is officially binding upon the faith of all Catholics, Revelation was closed with the death of the last Apostle. Of course God can and possibly does make revelations to individuals now living. However, the Pope or the Church cannot make such private revelations part of the *De Fide* Catholic Creed.

But though the deposit of faith was closed with the death of the last Apostle, our understanding of Revelation may grow. This accounts for the definition of additional dogmas, such as that of the Immaculate Conception of the Mother of Christ or of the infallibility of the Pope, as late as the nineteenth century. And it may be that other dogmas (as, for example, the Assumption of the Blessed Virgin) will be defined by the Pope or by a General Council at some future date. There is a certain development of doctrine for the Catholic Church.[1]

It should be said further that the inspiration of the canonical books of the Bible applies only to the original manuscripts. Hence, without harm to the belief in inspiration, textual errors may have been made in copying these original writings. The Church, however, guarantees to the faithful that the Latin version by St. Jerome, properly interpreted, does not teach error. At the same time, though, the Church admits that textual errors may have crept into the Vulgate, as this Latin translation is called. In fact, a biblical commission appointed by Pope Pius X

[1] *"Essay on the Development of Doctrine,"* by John Henry Newman, is the classical treatment of this subject in English.

has been working steadily on a revision of current editions of the Vulgate.

With the Catholic understanding of inspiration and the possibility of textual errors, the Bible offers no insoluble difficulties in the historical or scientific fields.

It is true that there was considerable controversy stirred up by Galileo in regard to the Copernican system. Galileo was condemned, but he was not tortured, and his prison was the palace of his friend the Grand Duke of Tuscany, at Rome, of his friend Archbishop Piccolomini, at Siena, and his own villa. "We readily grant," writes A. Tanquerey, in his text of dogmatic theology used in numerous Catholic seminaries for the priesthood, "that these Congregations were wrong in condemning Galileo . . . and that the two Popes (Paul V and Urban VIII) erred, not only as private persons, but as the heads of these Congregations, whose decrees were valueless unless approved by the Pope. But the decisions of the Congregations, even when approved by the Supreme Pontiff, are not infallible, unless the Pope makes them his own and promulgates them in his own name, with all the conditions necessary for an *ex cathedra* definition. This was not done in this case." [1]

The Bible is a collection of some hundred books written over a period of a thousand years by men with an oriental background in languages long since dead. Catholics believe that just as we need a final Supreme Court to decide between different interpretations of our federal constitution written only 150 years ago by men with substantially the same language and background as we have, so we need a teaching authority in the Church. That authority has decided for us just what books belong in the Bible, and as

[1] Theol. Dogmat., vol. I, p. 47, quoted in *"The Question Box,"* by Bertrand Conway. This is an inexpensive but excellent treatment of some thousand questions asked about the Catholic Church.

controversies in interpretation have from time to time arisen it has decided which contestant was right. Catholics do not believe that the ordinary individual Catholic is gifted by God with infallibility in interpreting the Scriptures. But they do believe that God has given infallibility to one individual, the Pope, in his official capacity as Head of the Church. When ordinary means of scholarship fail, he will decide between two or more interpretations.

The reverence of the Church for the Bible is shown by the safeguards she tries to throw around its use. She encourages Catholics to read the Bible by granting spiritual privileges to readers, but it must be an approved translation with notes. God's Revelation is so sacred that its vernacular presentation receives the most careful consideration by the Church.

Her reverence is also shown by the place the Bible (or selections from the Bible) occupies in her liturgy. The Catholic religion is a liturgical religion, that is, although it encourages the individual to pray directly to God, it provides a public worship of God according to prescribed forms. Of the liturgical forms, the Mass is unquestionably the greatest. It is for the Catholic the central act of worship of Our Lord sacramentally present, and a re-presentation of Christ's sacrifice on the Cross. And the Mass is thoroughly scriptural.

Masses vary from day to day. Although the words of consecrating the bread and wine are always the same, a repetition of Our Lord's words at the Last Supper, and there is a core called the "ordinary" of the Mass which is practically identical in all Masses, there are certain parts which vary according to the season or the feast. All Masses, however, are made up largely of selections from Scripture, both the Old and the New Testaments.

Except in a few Masses, for instance, Psalm XLII is said

at the beginning of every Mass (in the Roman rite). The Introit (first prayer read from the Missal) is a selection from the Bible, frequently from the Old Testament. There is a lesson, usually from one of the Epistles though sometimes from the Old Testament, and a passage from the Gospels, besides other scriptural selections.

That Catholicism and Judaism are two phases of the same divine religion is brought out by the commemoration of Saints of the Old Testament with Christian Saints in the same Mass, as the Machabees on August 1. In every Mass immediately after the consecration the celebrant prays God to look favorably upon the oblation just offered as He was pleased to accept the offerings of Abel, the sacrifices of Abraham and Melchisedech. Old and New Testament are so intimately interwoven in the Mass that their mutual dependence is clearly brought out.

The Roman Breviary, from which every priest who does not use a special Breviary—as the Benedictine—must read each day for about forty-five minutes, is made up almost entirely of passages from the Bible. Thirty-nine or forty Psalms are said each day, and so arranged that the whole Book of Psalms is read each week. In a year the lessons for the first nocturn are taken in order from every book of the Old Testament and of the New, thus giving a bird's eye view of the whole Bible.

Some sisterhoods have the same obligation that priests have of reading the Breviary, and a few pious laymen read it out of devotion. As has been said, laymen are encouraged to read the Bible, though the Church insists that the translation have a Catholic *imprimatur*. The English translation most in use is called the Douay or Rheims, because it was started in the sixteenth century by the English exiles at Douay and continued at Rheims. It was made from the Vulgate.

II. THE CATHOLIC CREED

1. General Summary

I BELIEVE in God, the Father Almighty, Creator of heaven and earth; and in Jesus Christ, His only Son, our Lord: who was conceived by the Holy Ghost, born of the Virgin Mary, suffered under Pontius Pilate, was crucified; died, and was buried. He descended into hell; the third day He arose again from the dead; He ascended into heaven, sitteth at the right hand of God the Father Almighty; from thence He shall come to judge the living and the dead. I believe in the Holy Ghost, the Holy Catholic Church, the communion of Saints, the forgiveness of sins, the resurrection of the body, and the life everlasting. Amen.

The Apostles' Creed printed above is the shortest and most used summary of Catholic belief. In the Sunday Masses, and other days that the Creed is said in the Mass, the Nicene Creed (formulated by the Council of Nice) is used. Converts on reception into the Catholic Church read the creed of Pope Pius V, which is considerably longer than the Apostles' or the Nicene Creeds.[1]

"I believe in God, the Father Almighty, Creator of heaven and earth," begins the Apostles' Creed. Naturally, believing in the Bible as the word of God, the Catholic religion must accept the delineation of God presented by the Old Testament. Whole books have been written on

1 These Creeds will be found conveniently in *The Manual of Prayers,* a standard Catholic prayerbook obtainable through any bookseller.

the attributes of God, and others on creation and evolution. The God of Catholicism is a personal God possessing intelligence and free will, and it is because we have intelligence and free will that we are said to be made in His likeness. Unlike us, however, God is a pure spirit possessing no body, and so is not subject to the limitations of matter.

God is infinite, possessing all perfections in an infinite degree. He is everywhere whole and entire; He is all good, and infinitely benevolent. God has always existed in one eternal now. For Him there is neither past nor future but only present—"I am who am." If time is a mystery to mathematicians, eternity is a still greater mystery. Our finite minds can never understand the infinite under any of its aspects.

God is all knowing. Nothing has happened or can happen in the universe without His knowledge, and it cannot happen without His concursus or cooperation in the sense that He keeps the temporal agents in existence. That is, everything except God is a contingent being. It might not have existed. God is a necessary Being, existing by the necessity of His nature. On this one non-contingent Being, God, all contingent beings depend for their existence. God is all powerful, can do anything, and since He is pure word He can do it merely by willing it.

Catholics are not blind to the difficulties involved in this theistic belief. The Church's theologians and philosophers have considered every objection ever thought of by atheist or agnostic; but also they have considered the difficulties involved in denying the existence of the Catholic's God.

One of the theistic difficulties, of course, is the existence of moral evil. How could an all-good, an all-benevolent, an all-powerful God bring into existence human beings knowing that some of them would rebel against His will and, dying in their wickedness, would suffer for all eternity in Hell? God has not revealed the answer, and the keenest human minds have been unable to solve the difficulty. Nevertheless, we can have faith in God's infinite goodness, and knowledge, and power. And at the same time we can see that the intellectual difficulties involved in denying God's existence are much greater than any difficulties posed by His infinity.

As Creator, Catholics believe, God brought the universe and everything in it into existence, and sustains it in existence. If it were not for the same omnipotent power put forth every moment to preserve creatures, all of them would lapse into the nothingness from which they came. But though the Catholic Church is irrevocably committed to the biblical account of creation, it is not committed to a literal interpretation of that account. A Catholic may believe that God created the universe in six days of twenty-four hours each; but, on the other hand, he may believe in any theory of evolution which safeguards the spirituality of the human soul and the idea of God as the ultimate First Cause. Likewise he may believe in Archbishop Usher's chronology of the Bible or in the latest scientific estimate of the age of the earth and of the human race.

The Nicene Creed puts very succinctly the Catholic belief in regard to the Incarnation and the Trinity: "And in one Lord Jesus Christ, the only begotten Son of God, born of the Father before all ages; God of God, true God of true God; begotten, not made. Who for us men, and for our salvation, came down from heaven and was incarnate by the Holy Ghost of the Virgin Mary, and was made man." A fuller and more explicit statement of the Catholic dogmas on the Trinity will be found in the Athanasian Creed.

Both the Trinity and the Incarnation are mysteries of faith—that is, no human mind can fully understand them. Just how there can be Three Divine Persons and only one God cannot be completely explained. All that can be done is to make a little clearer, perhaps, what we actually believe. We are, of course, staunch monotheists. We believe that there is only one God, and that only He is to receive divine worship; but we also believe that there are Three Persons in this one God, the Father, the Son, and the Holy Ghost, each co-equal with the other two.

When the first man, Adam, chosen by God as the representative of the human race, disobeyed God, he lost for himself and for his descendants the supernatural gifts which God had bestowed on him, especially the possibility of eternal happiness with God hereafter. This was the first or original sin, and an atonement for it was necessary. Each human being is said to be born with original sin, not in the sense that he commits this sin in the same way he commits other sins during his life, but in the sense that he does not have the supernatural gifts which he would have had if the representative of the race had been faithful to God.

The atonement for this first sin of Adam, and for all sins which human beings would ever commit, was accomplished by the Second Person of the Trinity becoming man and suffering death on the cross. He received His human body from Mary, but He had no human father. Catholics believe in the Virgin Birth of Our Lord; and in the Immaculate Conception of His Mother, Mary. That is, by an anticipation of the merits of her Son, Mary never suffered the stain of original sin, but came into existence as free from sin as did the first woman, Eve. We call Mary the Mother of God because Jesus, her Son, is God. But of course she is not in any way the author of the Godhead, and is not worshipped as God is worshipped.

Christ's crucifixion was for our sins today, as well as for Adam's sins, and for the sins of all men between Adam and ourselves. For the Catholic the important thing is that his own sins were responsible for Christ's death. Thus for the devotional practice of the Stations of the Cross—short meditations on incidents in Christ's passion—Cardinal Newman writes for the first station: "Jesus is condemned to *death.* His death-warrant is signed, and who signed it but I, when I committed my first mortal sins? . . . Those sins of mine were the voices which cried out: 'Let Him be crucified.' " And the same thought runs through innumerable sermons, meditations, treatises.

But the Second Person of the Trinity became man not only to die in atonement for human sins, but also to furnish us an example of perfect living and to give us additional Revelation of God. During His public ministry He chose certain Apostles who were to continue teaching His Revelation to all nations and to administer the Sacraments, which He had established. They and the disciples who accepted the new Revelation formed a true society, with head and members. One of them, Peter, had a primacy of governing and of deciding the correct interpretation of God's Revelation, as, for instance, in accepting gentiles into the society.

Though they are not all specifically mentioned in the Apostles' Creed, there is a supernatural help, a Sacrament, for each of the great experiences of life—seven in all. For birth there is Baptism; on attaining the use of reason, Confirmation—each to be received but once. Corresponding to the food for the body is the Eucharist, while the medicine for the soul curing the sickness of sin is the Sacrament of Penance. Under ordinary circumstance the Eucharist may be received as often as once a day; Penance may be received as often as desired. Marriage was raised by Christ to the dignity of a Sacrament and made indissoluble except by the death of one of the spouses. Those who devote themselves to the priesthood receive Holy Orders. Finally, for the last great adventure, the passing into eternity through death, there is for those who have obtained the use of reason and so can have sinned, the Last Anointing, or Extreme Unction.

Man has both a body, Catholics believe, and a soul. The body is subject to disease and death; the soul is immortal. Those who have received Baptism [1] and die without the stain of mortal sin will see God eternally. That sight of God is Heaven.

Those who die with their will completely turned away from God will suffer for all eternity the loss of the Beatific Vision, and the pain of this loss which they freely brought upon themselves is the essence of Hell.

Only absolutely pure souls can enter Heaven, and only those dying with unforgiven mortal sin go to Hell. Those who die with the stain of venial sin, or the remains of forgiven mortal sin, for a time endure a state, Purgatory, which is neither Heaven nor Hell, until they have been purged or purified for entrance into Heaven.

Catholic theology allows for degrees of sin. Some acts are such a slight digression from the right order that Catholics do not believe they incur the complete loss of man's last end, the Beatific Vision; and some acts, though in themselves a complete turning away from God, are

[1] For a statement as to how those who have not received Baptism of water may be said to have received Baptism, and so be saved, see p. 125.

not such for the agent because of his insufficient knowledge or insufficient consent of the will. They are called venial sins.

A mortal sin is the commission of some act which is in itself—or is thought by the agent at the time of acting to be—a complete turning away from God. The intellect must recognize it as seriously sinful and the will must fully consent to the act. For though man has free will, there may be circumstances reducing an individual's freedom below the completeness necessary for mortal sin.

This introduces the distinction between *formal* and *material morality*. Formal morality is the conception of the morality of an act in the mind of the agent at the time of acting; material morality is the act as it is objectively.

Thus a nurse, through no fault of her own, thinking that she was administering a healthful potion when in reality she was giving a deadly drink, would not be guilty of murder; whereas a nurse wishing to be rid of a patient, and with that intention giving what she thought was a deadly drink but which was really a helpful medicine, would be formally, though not materially, guilty of murder. Anything which lessens knowledge of the sinful character of the act or lessens consent of the will affects the formal morality of the act.

When one dies with one's will turned completely away from God, then one's will remains so for all eternity. In this sense it is not God who condemns a sinner to suffer for all eternity, but the sinner himself. On the other hand, till the last moment of life on earth it is, with grace, possible for the individual to turn back to God, and as a result to enjoy Heaven for all eternity. Essentially, Heaven is the activity of the intellect in knowing and of the will in loving God with faculties which have been freed from the limitations of a material body.

The phrase of the Apostles' Creed, "in the resurrection of the body," means that the body which has shared in the sins and virtues of the soul on earth will rise at the last day to share the soul's fate hereafter. It will not have the same characteristics of material extension which it has now, it will not be subject to sickness and death, it will not have the defects of the earthly body, and yet can be truly called the same body. We do not understand how this can be. But we can nevertheless sincerely recite the phrase of the Apostles' Creed, "I believe in the resurrection of the body."

One other statement of the Apostles' Creed deserves mention, "the communion of saints." The Church is made up of three broad divisions. One of these divisions is the Church militant, those souls still on earth who are fighting the good fight against temptations to sin. Those who profess the faith of Our Lord Jesus Christ, partake of His Sacraments, and submit to the authority of the Bishop of Rome are said to belong to the visible body of the Church militant. Excommunication bars the excommunicated person from the normal reception of the Sacraments. but it does not pretend to decide the eternal condition of that person. Those who believe in a Supreme Being as a rewarder and punisher and live up to their conscience, even though they do not belong to her visible organization, are said to belong to the invisible Church.

The Church suffering is composed of those souls who are now in Purgatory, being purified for their entrance into Heaven. They can be helped by the prayers and good works, we believe, of the Church militant.

The Church triumphant is those who have already attained the Beatific Vision. They are the saints with whom we believe that the Church militant and the Church suffering have communion, a "great crowd which no man could number," far more numerous than the known martyrs and those Saints declared by the Church on earth to have exercised such heroic virtue that they are surely in Heaven.

Catholics believe that members of the Church triumphant, whether canonized or not, can, by their intercession with God, help those still on earth. And so we Catholics pray to individuals of this Church triumphant, particularly the Mother of Christ. We pray, however, not as asking these Saints to help us by any power of their own, but asking them to pray to God to help us, as a son may ask a saintly living mother to pray for him. Catholics are convinced that if the prayers of those still on earth will avail, much more will the prayers of those in Heaven.

How do those in Heaven know that those on earth are asking their intercession? We do not know exactly. They know what God wants them to know, and we believe that God wants them to know this.

2. The Sacraments

BAPTISM. In general, a Sacrament is an outward sign of invisible grace established by Christ. All grace is a supernatural help given by God. Habitual or Sanctifying grace produces that condition in the soul by which it is pleasing to God and will receive eternal salvation; actual grace is given by God to enable the soul to meet particular occasions. A Sacrament of itself produces grace apart from the worthiness of the minister of the Sacrament. But the reception of the sacramental grace depends upon the recipient's dispositions.

The Sacrament which is first in time of reception is Baptism, because it is an initiation into the society or Church which Christ founded. And "unless a man be born again of water and the Holy Ghost, he cannot enter into the kingdom of God." (John, III, 5)

Baptism is so important that anyone may validly, and in case of necessity licitly, administer it. For Catholics the ordinary minister of Baptism is a priest, and in infant Baptism the pastor of the parish in which the parents have their domicile. Present practice in the Latin rite administers Baptism by pouring, but the Church recognizes the validity of Baptism by immersion or by sprinkling.

Because anyone can validly administer Baptism, the Catholic Church recognizes the Baptism received in a non-Catholic Church provided it can be proved to have lacked no essential element. These essential elements are that the minister of Baptism should have the intention of conferring the Sacrament according to the mind of Christ—and that the recipient who has attained the use of reason should intend to receive the Sacrament— should make natural water flow over the head or body of the person to be baptized while the minister (not someone else) says the words, "I baptize thee in the name of the Father, and of the Son, and of the Holy Ghost."

Besides the three methods of Baptism by water the Church admits Baptism of blood (martyrdom endured by an unbaptized person for Christ) and Baptism of desire. One who has faith and intends to receive Baptism of water, but who dies before actually receiving Baptism of water, receives Baptism of desire. Indeed, for Baptism of desire it is not necessary that the desire be explicit. If the person earnestly desires to do everything that he knows God wishes him to do, and would be baptized if he knew that

God wished him to be baptized, is perfectly sorry for his sins and loves God with perfect charity, then that person receives Baptism of desire, which has the same effect as Baptism of water. It removes all sin and confers sanctifying grace. Hence Baptism of desire is sufficient for salvation, and on the principle of Baptism of virtual desire even one who has never heard of Christ may be saved.[1]

For one with the use of reason to receive Baptism of water there must be faith in Jesus Christ and all that He taught. In addition, there must be sorrow for all one's sins. The sorrow need not be out of pure love for God, but it must be referred in some way to God.

It should be noted that to say Baptism is necessary for salvation, is not to say that those who die without Baptism, even Baptism of desire, will suffer the torments of Hell for all eternity. The souls whom Christ visited in Limbo between His death and resurrection were certainly not enjoying the Beatific Vision; but just as certainly they were not damned. It would seem that they were in a state of merely natural happiness, and it is possible that those who die without Baptism may enjoy such happiness.

Infants and imbeciles who have never enjoyed the use of reason may possibly in the moment of the soul separating from the body have a sufficient flash of intelligence to know that there is a God and desire to do everything that He wishes. In that case they would receive Baptism of desire. We do not know because God has made no Revelation on this particular point. We can only leave them to the uncovenanted mercies of an all-good God with the hope that the God who grants supernatural happiness to the repentant sinner, no matter how great his

[1] For a detailed consideration of all those groups who may, according to Catholic belief, be saved consult "A Doctrine of Hope," by Bishop Bonomelli.

crimes, will not do less for the soul who has never committed formal sin.

It is never assumed that a particular individual had such perfect love of God and sorrow for his sins that he received Baptism of desire, and that therefore Baptism of water need not be given. If possible, Baptism of water is administered, though Baptism of water can be received only once. Converts to Catholicism who have been baptized are baptized with the formula: "If you have never been baptized, then I baptize you," etc. This is not because only a Catholic can validly baptize, but because there may have been some invalidating circumstance in the first Baptism, as, for instance, the water being applied before or after the recitation of the words.

Baptism is necessary for the reception of any other Sacrament, and because Matrimony is a Sacrament one might untruly conclude that therefore Catholics do not recognize the marriage of unbaptized persons. Two unbaptized persons, who are otherwise free to marry, may contract a valid marriage, though they do not receive the Sacrament of Matrimony.

CONFIRMATION. At one time it was customary to give the Eucharist and Confirmation to infants, and in some places it is still customary to confer Confirmation on those who have not attained the use of reason. Generally, however, the recipient of Confirmation is able to distinguish between good and evil. By Confirmation he receives the Holy Ghost to enable him to resist the temptations which will inevitably come with life.

The ordinary minister of Confirmation is a bishop. But in unusual circumstances simple priests are sometimes empowered to confer Confirmation. The external sign of the inward grace is the anointing with episcopally blessed oil. Confirmation is not necessary for salvation, nor for the reception of any other Sacraments, although one should not neglect to receive it. Confirmation may not be received more than once. If the recipient needs more strength to meet the temptations of life, he may receive it through the Eucharist or through the Sacrament of Penance, both of which may be received more than once.

PENANCE. Confirmation is called a Sacrament of the living, that is, to receive it one should be in a state of grace, without the stain of original or of mortal sin upon his soul. Consequently, because the Sacrament of Penance is intended for the remission of sins, it is received, by those who have attained the use of reason, before Confirmation. The Sacrament of Penance is the Sacrament in which by confession of one's sins (with the proper dispositions of soul) to a duly authorized priest and the reception of his absolution one obtains the forgiveness of the guilt of one's sins. Every mortal sin committed since Baptism and not previously submitted to the forgiving power of the Sacrament of Penance must be confessed; if there is no such mortal sin, one may confess any mortal sin already forgiven by Baptism or by Penance, or one may confess any venial sin.

In confession one must accuse one's self of the number and kind of mortal sins one has committed since Baptism and not previously confessed. Any circumstance which changes the nature of a mortal sin—simple theft, for instance, to sacrilege—must be confessed. But sacramental confession should be restricted to the essentials and to one's own sins. For too great detail may do harm to the penitent, and he should not reveal the sins of another.

Intentionally to omit a mortal sin which should be confessed is in itself a mortal sin and renders useless the confession of other sins. But if one inadvertently forgets a mortal sin in confession, it is indirectly forgiven, and it is only necessary to mention it in one's next confession. One should strive for reasonable completeness in one's confession, and to attain that should spend a sufficient time in examining one's conscience. Forgiveness, however, depends upon God's mercy, not on the perfection of detail in confession. Scrupulosity and carelessness should both be avoided in confession.

There are, besides unblamable forgetting, other legitimate reasons for not confessing all sins. For instance, confession is auricular, and one who cannot speak is not bound to write a list of his sins. But he should indicate guilt and sorrow in a general way. Unconsciousness, of course, precludes even such a manifestation, and conditional absolution may be given under the formula, "if you have the proper dispositions."

In addition to a willingness to make a complete confession, the conscious penitent must have a supernatural sorrow for each and every mortal sin—that is, the motive for his sorrow must refer in some way to God. If he be sorry for his sins because by them he has offended an all-good God to whom he owes everything, the sorrow is perfect; if he be sorry for some more selfish reason, as because he must undergo a supernatural punishment for his sins, either on earth or in the next life, the sorrow is imperfect but supernatural, and, with the Sacrament of Penance, is sufficient to obtain God's forgiveness for any sin, no matter how grave nor how often committed. Sorrow that is not tied in with God at least thus selfishly, and so is in no way supernatural, is not enough, no matter how many times a priest's absolution may be obtained.

Imperfect sorrow of the supernatural kind explained

above ("attrition" it is called technically, as contrasted with "contrition" or perfect sorrow) is sufficient without the Sacrament of Penance to obtain God's forgiveness for venial sin. And there is no strict obligation to confess venial sins. Perfect sorrow without the Sacrament of Penance obtains God's forgiveness immediately for all sins both mortal and venial. But included in the perfect sorrow of a Catholic would be the intention of going to confession when reasonably convenient.

Sorrow is a matter of the will, not of the penitent's feelings and still less of the external gestures of his body. The penitent may be sincerely sorry out of pure love of God, and yet not feel sorrow in the same emotional way that he feels sorrow at the death of a beloved parent. Indeed, it is better for him not to try to make his sorrow emotional by asking himself if he would be willing to suffer this or that temporal loss rather than again offend God. For the things of this world are tangible, and he may find temporal things which he has experienced outweighing spiritual things which he has never experienced.

A Catholic who has no opportunity to receive the Sacrament of Penance, or a non-Catholic who does not, through no fault of his own, believe in confession, may obtain forgiveness through perfect sorrow. It is a matter of Catholic faith that those who die in mortal sin go to Hell, there to suffer for all eternity. But we cannot be sure that any particular individual did not at the last moment of his earthly existence have perfect sorrow.

Consequently the Catholic Church, though she has canonized many individuals, that is, solemnly declared that they lived a life on earth of such heroic virtue they are now in Heaven, has never declared that any individual, even Judas, died in mortal sin, and so now is in Hell.

Included in the true sorrow required for confession is a firm purpose of amendment, an intention of never offending God again. This must be universal and sovereign, extending to all sins and looking upon any temporal loss as preferable to sin. The penitent may deceive the confessor and get his absolution, but cannot deceive God. Unless in God's sight the penitent has the right kind of sorrow, the priest's absolution does him no good.

The penitent has not the right kind of sorrow unless he is willing to make restitution for injury which the penitent intentionally and unjustly caused anyone. This includes injury to reputation by slander or detraction as well as injury in material goods. Of course, no one is bound to do the impossible, and if a penitent *cannot* make restitution he is not bound to make it; but for absolution he must have at least the willingness to make restitution in case it should become possible.

One test of a resolution is that it should be kept, but it is not an infallible test. It is possible that one may have a genuine determination not to commit again a particular sin, and yet the temptation, when it comes, may prove too strong. If one has sinned often in a certain way, there has been built in the nervous system a channel which the same stimuli are inclined to follow to the same motor response as previously, and that habit of sin remains after confession. Generally speaking, to overcome a habit of reacting in a particular way a temptation must be overcome as often as it was previously followed. The Sacrament of Penance, although it produces grace, is not magic relieving the penitent of all effort. He must do his part, and the grace of the Sacrament is a help towards that end.

If a penitent fails in his resolution and yields again to temptation, he should not be so discouraged that he concludes there is no use trying. Rather he should make the best act of sorrow he can, and go to confession at the first opportunity. The Sacrament of Penance is for sinners, and the penitent who is in earnest can do better with the grace of the Sacrament than he can do without it. Consequently, the sinner should not stay away from confession with the idea that it is best not to confess until he has conquered his sins.

Before giving absolution, the priest imposes a penance on the penitent, and this must be accepted by the penitent for the valid reception of the Sacrament. In the early days of Christianity the penance was often quite severe, and probably for this reason the Sacrament is called Penance, rather than Confession or Absolution. As time went on, however, the custom arose of commuting the sacramental penance into something less severe. This was called a "commutation," and it is a great pity that the name was not kept. Today it is called an "indulgence."

An indulgence is not a permission to commit sin, nor absolution in advance of sin, but it is a commutation of the temporal punishment due to sin after the guilt has been forgiven. This is accomplished by the Church applying from her treasury of the merits of Christ and of the Saints sufficient to do what the performance of the sacramental penance under the earlier discipline would have done. Hence there are indulgences for 50 or 100 days. A plenary indulgence is the remission of the whole temporal punishment due to an individual's sins. By the communion of saints, we believe, an indulgence may be gained by a living person and applied to a soul in Purgatory, thus reducing its burden in that state of suffering.

In addition to the punishment for the guilt of sin, which in the case of mortal sin means the loss of Heaven, there is a temporal punishment which must be undergone either in this life or in Purgatory. The individual can voluntarily perform some penance now in order to avoid punishment in the future life, and some persons have more than satisfied for their sins. These merits and those of Christ form a treasury upon which the Church can draw. By the power of the keys "whatsoever you shall loose upon earth shall be loosed also in heaven" (Matt. XVIII, 18) the Church attaches some of these merits to a particular act or prayer, and what was before valueless acquires value from the merits of this spiritual treasury.

Church law prescribes confession at least once a year for those who have mortal sins to confess. The penitent is free to confess to any priest approved in the place where the confession takes place. The rule of religious communities usually requires weekly confession.

Ordinarily confession must be to a duly authorized priest. But in danger of death any priest, even an apostate, may licitly and validly hear the dying one's confession if no other priest is available. No priest, not even the Pope, may confess to himself. There is, of course, no fee or offering for confession. In some dioceses, indeed, it is strictly forbidden for a priest to accept any money, no matter for what purpose, in the confessional.

Sins are confessed to the priest as the representative of God. The strictest possible law binds him to secrecy. Outside the confessional he is not allowed, except with the permission of the penitent, to mention anything, even to the penitent himself, about what was confessed. Even to save his own life he may not break the seal of confession. In fact, he may not use information gained through confession to govern his external conduct in such a way as to imply that he is using such information.

THE EUCHARIST. When Our Lord at His Last Supper took bread and breaking it gave to His disciples saying, "Take ye and eat, for this is My Body," and similarly with the chalice, "This is the chalice of My Blood," we believe that the substance of the bread and of the wine was changed into the substance of the Body and of the Blood of Jesus. And when He added, "Do this in commemoration of Me," He gave to those Apostles and their successors the power of effecting the same change of the substance of bread and wine into the substance of the Body and Blood of Christ.

Technically, the doctrine is called transubstantiation—the passing of one substance into another substance. What is substance? That in which the accidents of taste, color, etc., inhere. Those accidents of bread and wine remain after consecration, but they then inhere in the substance of Christ's Body and Blood. It is a mystery how this can be and we shall never understand it fully. But that does not prevent our believing that Christ is present in some special way, other than the omnipresence of the Godhead, in the Eucharist.

It is the real Body and Blood of Our Lord which we take in Holy Communion. But since the accidents are those of bread, we are not eating the Body of Christ in any cannibalistic sense. That substance of the Body and Blood of Christ remains only as long as the accidents of bread and wine endure. When the accidents of bread and wine disappear, the Body and Blood of Christ are no longer present. Consequently the consecrated bread and wine are assimilated by the body of the recipient in the same way that unconsecrated bread and wine would have been assimilated.

The consecration of bread and wine (except consecration for Viaticum in case of necessity) takes place in the Mass. The essential words of the Mass are a repetition of Christ's words at the Last Supper, "This is My Body," "This is My Blood." Latin, with a few Greek and Hebrew words, is the language of the Mass for most of the priests of the Catholic Church.

However, eleven other languages are used by certain other groups (as in the case of the Maronites) in celebrating Mass, and the ceremonies of Mass differ according to twenty rites. Some of the rites vary little from the Roman, but others differ so much that they are almost as strange to a Roman rite Catholic as they are to a Methodist. However, the essence of the Mass, no matter what the rite, is the same.

The vestments of the Roman rite worn by the celebrant, although so strange to modern eyes, are simply the Roman garments of apostolic days modified somewhat through the centuries. To each, however, has been attached a symbolic meaning as indicated by the prayer which the priest says in donning it. Thus in putting on the chasuble, the last of the vestments, he says: "O Lord who has said, 'My yoke is sweet and My burden light,' grant that I may so carry it as to merit Thy grace." The chasuble, stole, and maniple are of the same color (red, white, green, purple, black) for the same Mass, but vary according to the time of the year or of the feast. Black is for requiem Masses.

The Mass is not only a re-enactment of the institution of the Eucharist at the Last Supper, it is also a re-presentation of the sacrifice of Christ on the cross to His heavenly Father. Hence the Mass has great values of satisfaction, worship, and petition. Every priest is bound to say Mass at least several times a year. He may say only one Mass a day, except that on Sundays he may, with the Ordinary's permission, say two, and by general law three on All Souls and Christmas.

The Mass is a public act of worship which the faithful who have attained the use of reason are bound to attend on Sundays and holy days of obligation. But, as has been said, no ecclesiastical law binds under a proportionately serious inconvenience, and there are many circumstances which excuse the individual from attendance at Mass. Mere bodily presence is not enough to fulfill the obligation—there must be some worship of God, though the individual may use any one of several recognized ways of assisting at Mass. Some say prayers, some meditate on the mysteries of the Mass or of religion in general, some sing hymns, some read to themselves in English or some other language the words the priest is reciting at the altar.

Certain prayers of the Mass are said alternately by the priest and the people, or the server representing the people. In a sung Mass the choir sings certain parts.

What Catholics believe in regard to the Mass is stated succinctly in *The New Catholic Dictionary:* "The Mass is identical with the Sacrifice of the Cross in the Victim and the Priest, which is Christ. On the Cross He offered Himself in person and in a bloody manner. As He offered up His death while consecrating the bread and wine, the priest also, acting in remembrance of Him, offers up His death at the consecration of the Mass. He is mystically slain in the separate consecration of bread and wine; the offering is perfected in the Communion of the priest. The value of this offering is infinite from the application of the merits of Christ's Passion and Death, giving adequate praise and thanksgiving to God. Inexhaustible also are its fruits as satisfaction for sins and punishment due them, and for obtaining all benefits. These fruits are applied partly by the will of the Church, partly by the intention of the priest offering, and partly by those devoutly assisting, for both the living and the dead."

Therefore an individual may have a Mass celebrated with the understanding that the priest celebrating will offer it for the individual's intention. But no individual can monopolize all the fruits of a Mass. Thus a pastor must say Mass for his congregation on Sundays and holy days of obligation, even on those days which are no longer but which once were holy days of obligation. Also there is a memento for all the faithful living and departed in every Mass, and many of the other prayers are so worded as to include everyone. Even in a funeral Mass for a dead Pope, the final prayer, just before the last Gospel, is in the plural, "May they rest in Peace"; when, if ever, one would expect an exclusiveness for the deceased whose dead body is present.

The Body and Blood of Christ, since it is a living Christ, are present whole and entire under the appearances of bread and the appearances of wine. Those who receive these appearances (whether of bread only, or of bread and wine) receive the whole Body of Christ. One communicant does not receive one part and another communicant another part, nor is it necessary to receive both bread and wine. Holy Communion, as the reception of the Sacrament of the Holy Eucharist is called, may be distributed during Mass or, when there is reason, outside of Mass, from the Hosts reserved in the tabernacle.

Under the present practice, Holy Communion is given only to those who have the use of reason, and who understand the fact of Our Lord's sacramental presence. But at one time Communion was given to infants under the form of wine, and in some Roman Catholic rites it is given under the form of both bread and wine. Communion is taken to the sick, and when administered to the dying under a special formula it is called "Viaticum."

To receive the Eucharist worthily—although of course no one can really be worthy of this gift of God—one should be in a state of grace, that is, without mortal or original sin, and, except for the sick, fasting from anything which is assimilated since midnight of the night before. It is perfectly lawful for a Catholic of the Roman rite to receive Communion under the form of bread and wine in those Roman Catholic rites giving Communion in this way.

Holy Communion may be received any number of times up to once a day. The only exceptions are the priest who says more than one Mass on the same day and one who having already received Communion becomes suddenly in danger of death through sickness and receives Viaticum. By canon law those who have made their first Holy Communion are obliged to receive Communion at least once a year during the Easter time—in this country from the first Sunday of Lent until Trinity Sunday.

Because the Body and Blood of Our Lord are present as long as the appearance of bread and wine remain in the consecrated species, we believe that Christ is sacramentally present in those churches where the Host is reserved. For that reason we genuflect before the tabernacle on entering or leaving church. Wherever the Eucharist is reserved a light, called the sanctuary lamp, is kept burning night and day.

Catholics are glad to have those who do not believe with them attend Mass. But Holy Communion is given only to Roman Catholics. And though Catholics when they have sufficient reason, as the funeral or marriage of some friend, may attend services in other than Roman Catholic churches, they should not take formal part in non-Catholic worship. Indeed, they could not take formal part in a worship directly stating—or even only implying—that Christ is not God, or that He is not really present in the Eucharist, or that He did not establish a Church with supreme teaching and governing authority, without being false to Christ and to their deepest convictions of what He taught.

In the same way, though Catholics expect visitors to Catholic churches to behave respectfully, they do not want them to take formal part in ceremonies belying their deepest convictions. They give to others, as does God Himself, the freedom to hold their own beliefs. The Catholic position is that no one should act against his conscience. A child is not baptized a Catholic unless his parents or guardians wish him to be and profess their intention of rearing him a Catholic. No priest may licitly receive into the Catholic Church one who acknowledges that he wishes to join merely for marriage or for some other worldly reason, but who has no conviction that he is morally bound to become a Catholic.

Holy Communion is not a necessary means for salvation, but those who are in earnest will not neglect to receive the Eucharist frequently. In the long history of the Church, ideas of what is proper frequency have varied considerably. Most religious and some layfolk receive Communion every day.

MATRIMONY. The Sacrament of Matrimony is the marriage of two baptized persons. Unbaptized persons, in the eyes of the Church, may be truly married, but because Baptism is a prerequisite for receiving any other Sacrament, they do not receive the Sacrament of Matrimony.

Canon law on marriage has varied from time to time. Under the present legislation a Catholic, when possible, must for validity marry before a pastor acting in his parish or a priest delegated by him (or by the Ordinary) and two witnesses. If for one month it has been impossible for a particular couple to have a priest assist at their marriage (as, for instance, on account of too great distance), they may marry validly and licitly before two witnesses. In any case, the priest is merely an official witness. The contracting parties are the ministers of the Sacrament of Matrimony. Hence the priest does not marry them, but they marry themselves.

We believe that Christ raised marriage to the dignity of a Sacrament and made it indissoluble except by the death of one of the parties. Therefore, in the case of *valid Christian consummated marriage* there is no divorce from the bond of Matrimony, though for a sufficient reason there may be a separation. If the marriage is merely ratified and not consummated there may be a divorce from the bond of marriage. Or if both parties are unbaptized, and, on the conversion of one spouse the other refuses to live peaceably, the Pauline privilege (mentioned in I Cor. X, 13) may be applied.

One of the primary ends of marriage is the propagation of the race, "to people Heaven," as an old prayer for those just married expresses it. But the Catholic attitude towards marriage does not imply that married folk should have as many children as physically possible. They must not, however, do anything in a chemical or mechanical or onanistic way to prevent conception. Still less is it lawful to contrive abortion.

Besides the lack of the necessary witnesses ("clandestinity"), there are other invalidating impediments in the eyes of the Church. It sometimes happens, therefore, that an invalidating impediment is discovered after the marriage ceremony before a priest. If the impediment can be dispensed by the Church, a dispensation may be obtained. But until the dispensation has been obtained, the marriage from a Catholic standpoint is null and void.

Hence if the parties to this supposed marriage had secured a civil divorce, then either would be free, after a declaration from the proper ecclesiastical authority that the previous supposed marriage was void, to marry elsewhere. That would not be a divorce from the Church, but a declaration of nullity.

Marriage, of course, is one field in which the Church and the State come into frequent contact. With the exception of South Carolina, every State in the Union grants divorces for reasons which the Catholic Church does not consider legitimate. Also, some of the States have established invalidating impediments going beyond those of canon law, and on the other hand do not recognize some of the impediments established by the Church. Therefore it can easily happen that persons are married in the eyes of the State but not in the eyes of the Church, or vice versa. Is there a conflict here between Church and State?

There is a difference, and we Catholics wish the difference could be removed. But there is no real conflict. Catholics whose marriage is valid in the eyes of the Church, but invalid in the eyes of the State, can remedy the condition before the State or else abide by the civil results which follow from the State law.

A real conflict between Church and State would require that the State should command Catholics to do what the Church forbids; or that it should forbid Catholics to do what the Church commands. This situation does not arise in regard to differences in marriage legislation between the Church and State. For the State merely says to Catholics: "You may marry So-and-So though your Church forbids you, and I shall support you in getting the civil rights of marriage." And, on the other hand, although the Church may recognize as an invalidating impediment to future matrimonial attempts a marriage which by the State law was invalid, she never says to her subjects: "You *must* marry though the State forbids."

The Church prefers that Catholics should marry Catholics. However, as a loving and practical mother, she recognizes that there may be reasons justifying a particular Catholic in marrying one who is not a Catholic. As an illustration of her sweet reasonableness, two of the conditions she accepts as justification are that the woman is over twenty-three, or that the place is so small eligible Catholics are few.

In applying for a dispensation the person who is not a Catholic signs promises to allow any children of the marriage to be baptized as Catholics and not to interfere with the practice of Catholicism by the Catholic party. Some dioceses require non-Catholics contemplating marriage with a Catholic to take some instructions in Catholicism, not with the intention of becoming Catholics, but that they may understand what they are promising. Decisions on the problems about which promises are made must be arrived at before or after marriage, and it seems better to meet the problems frankly before marriage, rather than to wait until they may occasion family disagreements.

HOLY ORDERS. Catholics believe that the ceremony of Holy Orders by which a bishop ordains a priest is a Sacrament leaving an indelible mark on the soul of the recipient. Hence, like Baptism and Confirmation, it can be received only once. The inherent power of the priesthood remains forever in one who has received Holy Orders, and that power may be exercised legitimately even by an apostate in case of extreme necessity. Thus any priest, if a dying man cannot have recourse to one with proper jurisdiction, may licitly confer upon the dying person the Sacrament of Penance.

Apart from such cases of extreme necessity, however, a priest must have the approval of the Ordinary to preach, jurisdiction from the Ordinary to absolve, delegation from a pastor (or, naturally, the Ordinary) to assist at a marriage. The right to give Confirmation may be, and sometimes is, granted by the Pope to a priest, but generally only Bishops give the Sacrament of Confirmation. The legislation is somewhat complicated, but the right to use the powers of the priesthood is further affected by the right of a pastor to confer Extreme Unction and Baptism on his own parishioners, to give them Viaticum, and to assist at their marriages.

The subdiaconate and diaconate are Major Orders. Usually those who receive them go on to the priesthood, and a priest has received them before the priesthood, just as a bishop has received the priesthood before receiving the episcopate. A bishop needs consecration by another bishop. He receives certain powers (as to ordain) which do not belong to the priesthood, but he does not receive another Sacrament of Orders.

The Sacrament of Holy Orders acts as an invalidating impediment to Matrimony. In the Latin rite priests are celibates; in some Eastern Churches united with Rome a priest may be married, but may not marry. That is, a married man may be ordained, but if his wife dies he may not marry again. Holy Orders is an impediment to Matrimony only by ecclesiastical law. The church could abrogate the law, or in individual cases dispense from it.

EXTREME UNCTION. If possible a sick person receives the Sacrament of Penance just before receiving Extreme Unction; but if that be impossible the Sacrament of Extreme Unction itself effects the remission of sins, provided the recipient has the proper dispositions. It is an anointing of the eyes, ears, nose, mouth, hands, and in the case of men, feet, with oil blessed on Holy Thursday by a bishop, while the priest says certain prayers.

As has been said, the right to administer Extreme Unction belongs to the pastor of the parish. He is bound to administer it to the sick, even at great danger to himself. Those responsible for the care of the sick should call the priest in ample time. The recipient of Extreme Unction must have reached the age of reason and be in danger of death through sickness, though the danger need not be acute. Extreme Unction may be received more than once, but only once for the same danger of death.

Preferably one should have the use of one's senses when anointed. But if one has become unconscious one may nevertheless be anointed, and if one had the proper dispositions on becoming unconscious the Sacrament will be effective. Even after apparent death, Extreme Unction may be administered because it is sometimes difficult to determine the exact moment of death.

III. CATHOLICISM IN THE LIFE OF CATHOLICS

1. The Private or Interior Life

CATHOLICISM should be like the Gospel leaven hid in three measures of meal. It should influence every part of life, interior and exterior. A Catholic should be better because of his Catholicism than he would be if he were not a Catholic.

But the Church is made up of good, bad, and indifferent men, as Christ, by several parables, taught that she would be, and she suffers all to grow until the harvest. It is only in exceptional cases that she excommunicates any individual by name, and even then the door for his return is always open.

In writing of the Catholic religion in the life of Catholics there is not intended any implication that all who call themselves Catholics fully use the possibilities of Catholicism in their living. But some do use the advantages afforded by Catholicism, and the possibilities are there for all.

It seems reasonable, therefore, to speak of what Catholicism could be in the lives of Catholics, without making any attempt to evaluate how far such possibilities are realized. Myriads of Catholics have wisely used their religion "to grow into the fullness of the stature of Christ" (Eph. IV, 13); though it must be frankly admitted that many Catholics with whom the reader may be acquainted seem to be cockle rather than wheat. The following pages try to draw an inadequate picture of how the Catholic who wishes can live Catholicism.

Ideally the moulding of a Catholic begins almost at birth. Baptism should not be unnecessarily delayed, but there are other ways in which the Catholic life should begin to function for the infant. As his eyes become accustomed to the light and able to distinguish objects, some of the first things he sees should have a religious association. Perhaps a cross or medal is on a chain around his little neck, or he amuses himself by playing with the cross dangling from his mother's necklace.

On the walls will be a crucifix and holy pictures, on the mantle or a little oratory will be statues of Our Lord and His Blessed Mother and St. Joseph. The Christmas tree will be associated not only with toys and gifts, but at its foot will be a reproduction of the crib at Bethlehem. Among the first words he learns will be Jesus, Mary, Joseph. And as he becomes able to speak, the Lord's prayer and the Hail Mary will be taught him, and their recitation will become part of his morning and evening routine.

Long before he is obliged by Church law to attend Mass on Sunday he will at times have been taken to church for Mass and for special devotions, such as Benediction. Strange vestments, aromatic censers, numerous lighted candles, flower-decked altar will all attract his childish attention. He will ask questions, giving the opportunity for teaching important truths, even the beginning of something about the Eucharist.

It is through this externalization of religion by the Catholic Church, and the grace of which she is a channel, that Our Lord, God the Father, the Saints, and Angels—

the whole supernatural world—become as real to a Catholic as is his own family, in fact are part of his family. Even before he has heard the phrase of the Apostles' Creed, "the communion of saints," he has realized its meaning, has prayed to the persons represented by the pictures and statues with which he has become familiar. The Infant Jesus is more real to him than fairies are to other children.

There are Catholic homes in which family prayers take place every day, and more homes in which they occur during special seasons, such as Lent or May. Such a practice is doubtless more difficult under present day conditions than it was before the radio and automobile, but it is still the ideal for the head of the family to read a little of the Bible each evening for the family and to recite a few prayers in unison. In a few Catholic parishes evening prayers are said in the church throughout the year.

Like other religions, Catholicism is not merely the recitation of prayers or creeds. It is also a keeping of the Ten Commandments. That is a matter of the will, and so from the very beginning of life the individual's will should be trained. Even before the infant can talk or walk, he can be made to understand that his desires are not supreme, but that many times he must conform himself to another's will. Mark Twain says that his first lie was pretending something was the matter with him so he would be taken up and fondled. Contrariwise, by not yielding to every whimper, and by never themselves lying to him, parents can gradually teach the infant to be truthful and obedient.

From a natural standpoint, truthfulness and obedience are perhaps the greatest touchstones of character. There is good foundation for hope that the child who has been thoroughly drilled in these virtues will grow up able to overcome the temptations of life. Practicing these virtues is not a mere memorizing of the Decalogue or of questions in the catechism, but a way of life. It is much more difficult to train children in habits of virtue than it is to get them to recite formulas glibly, but it can be done. By themselves setting an example of virtue, by judicious praise and blame administered with love, by prudence—which means, in addition to other things, avoiding priggishness—holding up the example of others tactfully, parents can train their children in a religious way of life, in a practice of both the natural and the supernatural virtues.

The truly religious child will be a well-mannered child. It is true that one can acquire good manners without religion, but one who has the fundamental bases of religion will find innumerable applications of religion in good manners. For one who has a real love of neighbor politeness will be a second nature. Cardinal Newman said that a gentleman never unnecessarily causes pain to another, and one who loves his neighbor, though he may not know which fork to use for a particular dish at a formal dinner, will certainly not cause unnecessary pain or inconvenience. Religion is the best basis for such unselfishness. Hence one finds oftentimes in poor, uncultured, unlettered Catholics an innate courtesy which is a product of their religion.

As the child gets older little lessons in unselfishness will be inculcated, and his mind will be prepared for the day—the completion of his seventh year—when he becomes subject to the law of Friday abstinence. At first his moral world will be to conform to what his parents wish, and his conception of sin will be to disobey them. But there will soon be added to this the idea of God as a Father, and sin will take on the complexion of disobeying God. When he acquires the use of reason and can distinguish between moral right and wrong, he will make his first confession. Naturally, he will have no serious sins to confess, but he will become accustomed to the obligation of confession; and as he grows older the advice he is given in the confessional, coupled with the knowledge that serious sin must be confessed, may preserve him from contracting habits which gradually lead on to serious sin.

> "The course of evil begins so slowly and from such slight source
> An infant's hand might stop the breach with clay.
> But let the stream grow larger, and Philosophy,
> Ay, and Religion, too, shall strive in vain
> To stem the headlong torrent."

Confession can enable the child to stop the course of evil while it is still easy to do so. The worst crimes of the most hardened criminal began in a small way. Teach the little boy to be careful in regard to little sins, and we may hope that he will grow up to be a virtuous man; just as the youth who is trained in habits of thrift will probably in adult life be financially careful and prudent. Of course, there is a miserly excess which goes to an extreme, and in morals there is a scrupulosity and priggishness. They should be avoided, for virtue is a mean between extremes.

But a reasonable tact and judgment can avoid such pitfalls, at the same time that it successfully quashes the beginning of bad habits. Confession at an early age can be, and often is, a natural as well as a supernatural help in preserving virtue. As the twig is bent, the tree's inclined; and confession gives the right support to rectitude.

At the time of his first confession or shortly after will come the child's first Holy Communion—the reception of the sacramental presence of that little Infant he has seen represented in the crib of Bethlehem, that Savior he has seen depicted dying for him on the cross, that Incarnate God, Jesus, whose life story in its various phases he has often heard.

Undoubtedly the story of the crucifixion could be told in such a way as to arouse in the child hatred for those who perpetrated the deed. But it can be safely said that the typical Catholic way is directed towards begetting sorrow for one's own sins rather than any animosity for others. For Christ was God as well as man, and therefore He would not have died in this way if He had not chosen to do so. The slightest suffering of the Second Person of the blessed Trinity was in itself sufficient to atone for Adam's sin and all other human sins, as well as to win back for us the possibility of being happy with God for all eternity. Our Lord chose to die on the cross to show us His love and His horror for sin.

Therefore the Catholic thought in meditating on the crucifixion is not turned towards hating the human instruments of 1900 years ago or their supposed descendants today, but towards loving a Savior who underwent so much for us. A hatred of his own sins, a willingness to avoid whatever is displeasing to such a Savior should be a product of the story of the crucifixion for every Catholic.

In every Catholic church there is a crucifix and in most there are fourteen bas reliefs or pictures representing various incidents in Christ's passion, called the "Stations of the Cross."

Also, there are usually in Catholic churches pictures and statues of other incidents in the life of Our Lord, or of His Blessed Mother, or of some Saints. Interwoven in the decoration of the Church are religious symbols and texts of Scripture in a frank and telling attempt to use the external to emphasize the truths of religion. So numerous were the Scriptural representations that John Ruskin, who was not a Catholic, called the cathedral of the town, "The Bible of Amiens."

At about the same time that he makes his first Holy Communion, the Sacrament of Confirmation will confer upon the child the gifts of the Holy Ghost to meet the increasing temptations of life and to practice the virtues of maturity. If the child corresponds, he will grow in ability to recognize within himself the impulses of the Holy Spirit in the various circumstances of life.

The will of God, expressed broadly in the Ten Commandments, may have an additional meaning for each individual. After Confirmation more especially God the Holy Ghost is speaking in the individual soul, gently leading him to do some things not required of everyone, to give up some things which in themselves are perfectly lawful. There will come a time when the individual Catholic must decide whether he (or she) is called to a serving of God in marriage or a dedication of one's service to God in the priesthood or in some religious community.

If a Catholic marries, it should not be through lust, but through the highest kind of conjugal love, in which natural inclinations are sublimated in the higher end of doing God's will, of acting as His agent in peopling Heaven, in giving to the new creatures of God the careful religious training which will insure the attainment of God's ultimate aim for human beings—the enjoyment by them of the Beatific Vision.

Concurrently with an exposition of Catholicism in the home and church will come a deepening of understanding through one's own efforts in reading and thinking. A knowledge of religion should keep pace with advancing maturity and with one's knowledge of profane subjects. "When I became a man, I put away the things of a child," wrote St. Paul (I Cor. XIII, 11). And similarly, an educated Catholic should so mature his conception of Catholicism that it will stand the strain of modern life.

A Catholic should not be content with fragments of the Gospels and Epistles heard from the pulpit on Sunday, but if he reads secular books and newspapers he should also read some religious books and papers. Above all, he should have his own personal copy of the Scriptures which he can mark to suit himself. He should have read the whole Bible at least once, and the New Testament several times, underlining favorite passages, making notes in the margin and flyleaves.

In addition to the Book of books, he should know some of the religious writings which have stood the test of time and have been reprinted in innumerable editions, such as Thomas à Kempis, *The Imitation of Christ;* St. Francis de Sales, *Introduction to a Devout Life;* Brother Lawrence, *Practice of the Presence of God;* Drexelius, *Heliotropium.* One could easily add dozens of titles to the list, and anyone not a Catholic who wants to know what Catholicism really is should know something of the great spiritual books which Catholics have produced.

Many devout Catholics follow the Mass with their own Missals. But even without a Missal no one can assist at Mass without absorbing a certain amount of Catholic culture. This great central act of worship has colored life for Catholic civilizations. It has inspired some of the finest art of the world in painting, sculpture, architecture, music.

The Roman Missal is itself a great work of literature, and connected with the Mass we have the wonderful churches of every century of the Christian era, from Sancta Sophia in the sixth century to the cathedral of Westminster in our own. The painting and sculpture of the greatest artists have adorned these churches with the theme of the Incarnation, and the perpetuation of the Incarnation in the Eucharist. The greatest musicians have delighted to write Masses.

In the Solemn Mass with its various incensings, an appeal to every sense has been used to achieve the one result of drawing the worshipper closer to God. For those with even a modicum of sympathy and understanding for the sublime subject matter of the Mass it is the most marvellous drama, not excepting the classic Greek, which human genius has ever united the arts to expound.

The central fact, the one that really counts without the artistry gathered round it, is the re-presentation in the Mass of Christ's sacrifice for man's redemption. But the Mass is more than that. Through its variable parts it is a re-presentation of Our Lord's life on earth from His birth on Christmas Day to His Ascension. And it is also a recapitulation of God's dealing with men from the creation of Adam, the sacrifices of Abel, Abraham, Melchisidech to the latest Saint to be raised to the altars of the Church. The athletes of Christ, the "knights and ladies of the Holy Spirit," are commemorated in the proper prayers of their Masses by some telling phrase which holds up to the faithful their special virtues for admiration and imitation.

Every personal and social condition confronting the Catholics of today, whether war, or persecution, or sickness, or poverty, has been met by some saintly predecessor from whose life, commemorated in the Mass, we can take courage.

Naturally, one cannot have at home the same union of

all the arts that one may have in a great church. But one can show that he is a Catholic by a picture or two, the books and magazines one has, and has not. In the morning, one's first thoughts should be of God. Even before one rises, one should offer the works and crosses of the day to God, and everything which happens to one should be accepted as coming from God. Therefore one's life should be a continuous litany of that phrase of the Lord's prayer, "Thy will be done!"

In fact, in spite of the seeming complexity of the Catholic religion and its frank use of externals, the essence of Catholicism can be summed up in that one phrase, "Thy will be done!" Everything in the Catholic Church, though to an outsider it may seem distracting and irrelevant, is directed to the purpose of bringing the human will into conformity with the divine will. The essence of sin consists in the individual setting his will against God's will; and, contrariwise, the essence of virtue consists in the individual making God's will his own.

The will is the faculty of loving, and we love God in the proportion that we turn towards Him with our will. Love of this infinite and all-perfect God is the highest possible exercise of the human will. To know God with our intellect and to love Him with our will, not as now with all the limitations imposed upon us by our clayey bodies but directly as one spirit knows another, is Heaven—the Beatific Vision.

Also, of course, God is intellect, and we must not emphasize one divine attribute at the expense of another. But God's will and various aspects of that will are certainly central to the Catholic religion. We are surely allowed to underline will as love to the extent that St. Paul does in his famous and sublimely beautiful Thirteenth Chapter of First Corinthians. "If I should have all knowledge and have not charity, I am nothing." We can know the summary of God's will as formulated in the Decalogue, but if we do not conform our will to God's will our knowledge avails us nothing. Hence the Catholic religion emphasizes the place of desire. Evil desires, acts of the will, are sinful. Not only wrong external actions, but also wrong internal desires, must be avoided.

Tied in with this question of the will is such a simple thing as Friday abstinence, and, indeed, all ascetical practices. "I chastise my body," says St. Paul elsewhere, "and bring it into subjection: lest perhaps when I have preached to others, I myself should become a castaway." (I Cor. IX, 27). The Church encourages a giving up of what is itself not wrong, provided such renunciation does not go to extremes, and provided it does not confuse the giving up of what is itself good with the avoidance of what is evil. She does not preach a dour, gloomy, morbid outlook on life. Those who are ascetic in the right way are among the happiest of mortals. They have life and life more abundant. St. Francis, giving up many of the good things of this world, found himself brother to all men and all things, a joyous troubadour of God. Joyousness is a note of true religion.

The clear distinction between the essential and the non-essential, and that God in addition to His general will expressed in the Decalogue has a special will for each individual, should keep one from ever being priggish. And the knowledge that God tolerates so much should lead the individual to a broad tolerance which makes for a happy association of human disparates instead of for a narrow insistence on absolute conformity.

Consider, too, how a conformity of the human will with

the divine produces a serene calm in facing the difficulties of life. Because God is omniscient, He knows just how the laws with which He endowed the universe will work out. The individual wants sunshine on a particular day, and instead gets rain. If he has truly grasped the fact of the universe and everything in it being contingent, then rather than feeling grouchy about the weather he accepts whatever it is cheerfully as in some way a manifestation of God's will. Even the forward actions of others toward him can be performed only by power in which God, the one necessary Being, momentarily sustains the human contingent agent. It is a mystery, but nevertheless a profound truth, that nothing can happen except by God's will or by God's permission. Therefore everything should be accepted as from God.

But Catholicism is not an introspective religion, whose greatest sanctity is Nirvana. It may be that the individual, though maintaining patience, should react vigorously to adverse circumstances instead of sitting listlessly with folded hands. Catholicism holds tenaciously to the two truths: that everything in this contingent universe depends upon the one non-contingent Being, God; and at the same time that men have free will with which to shape their destiny. Catholic Saints, as Francis of Assisi, Ignatius Loyola, Vincent de Paul, were among the most active characters in the world.

The externalism of the Catholic Church is evident to every observer. A Catholic is bound to attend the liturgical public worship of Mass every Sunday, he is encouraged to say vocal prayers every day, he receives certain outward signs in the Sacraments, he venerates the relics of the Saints, he uses the sign of the cross, holy water, and other sacramentals. But the spiritual benefit for him of any of these things depends upon his own inner disposition.

And a balance is kept between the external and the inner spirit. For the Catholic is also encouraged in a direct cultivation of the interior life through mental prayer as contrasted with vocal prayer. Members of religious communities have by their rule a certain time set aside each day for meditation on the truths of religion, the incidents of Christ's life, the application of Christ's example to themselves. Lay Catholics are also encouraged to practice such meditation and to make a retreat of several days when they separate themselves as far as possible from all worldly distractions. "The Spiritual Exercises" of St. Ignatius [1] are the classic expression of meditations for such retreats.

A few Catholics in each age have gone on to the heights of contemplation and experiential knowledge of God. One's knowledge of Catholicism is not complete until one has read some writings of the great mystics. *Sancta Sophia,* by Francis Baker is a good introduction to such literature. *The Mansions of the Soul,* by St. Teresa of Avila and *Dark Night of the Soul,* by St. John of the Cross, are two books which those interested in the mystical side of Catholicism should by all means read.

Without being morbid about it, a Catholic should realize his mortality and always be prepared for death. The ideal attitude is illustrated by an incident told of St. Aloysius. Aloysius and some companions were playing checkers when one of the group asked what they would do if they knew they would die in fifteen minutes. Aloysius replied that he would keep on playing. And if one has led the life of an Aloysius, then he can meet death in the same blithe way.

Not everyone, however, is a Saint, and it is natural for Catholics to wish to receive Penance, Viaticum, and the

[1] Cf. U. S. Catalogue for various editions.

Last Anointing as an immediate preparation for passing into eternity. Though Extreme Unction can be administered only to those in danger of death through sickness, it sometimes has a curative effect on the body and helps in the recovery of health. At any rate, it has a soothing, pacifying influence on the individual and enables him to face without fear the ordeal of dying.

Because Catholics believe that Extreme Unction is a Sacrament, a great spiritual help to Catholics in their passage into eternity, they expect non-Catholics with whom they are associated in sickness, to cooperate in securing for them the ministrations of a priest. As has been noted, there must be some danger of death for the administration of Extreme Unction, but the priest should be called before the danger of death is really acute and the sick person loses consciousness.

We have spoken of Catholicism as the help it can be for living to those who cooperate. But some, unfortunately, do not cooperate. There are Catholics who are among the big sinners of the world. What of them? Jesus reiterated the mercy of God in many a parable, *par excellence* in that of the Prodigal Son. Moreover, He showed that divine mercy when He forgave Mary Magdalen, and the thief on the cross, and built His Church on Peter who had thrice denied Him.

Someone once wrote a letter which was supposed to be an unanswerable attack on the Catholic Church, but which in reality brings out what the Church thinks is the mercy of Christ: "You talk about the purity and holiness of your church, but I remember that a priest was with Ruth Snyder, adulteress, murderess, and belated convert to the 'Church' when she paid with death the penalty for her guilty life. A priest went up to the scaffold with Hickman, the beast, who cut a little girl to bits, and then rushed converted into the arms of 'Holy Church.' Priests tear through the city when the pistols of gangland are out, and receive the last frightened sobs of the thug who was murdered by his kind. Your church loves to sweep up the refuse of the death cells and makes grand-stand play of snatching, on the steps of the gallows, another soul from hell. Gangsters and bootleggers, condemned murderers and dying prostitutes—of such is the holy and spotless Catholic Church."

That, too, is part of the picture of the Catholic Church. But as Father Lord, a Jesuit, said in his pamphlet, "Prodigals and Christ," from which the above letter is taken: "Even on his deathbed the sinner need not cry, 'Too late!' From the scaffold where he is meeting a deserved death, the soul of the murderer may find its way safely to God. Every priest in the world holds it high honor to snatch from the hands of the executioner a blood brother of the Good Thief whom Christ thought worthy to be His companion into eternity."

Catholicism is a religion for living, but also for dying. It comforts and strengthens those who have to die and those who must live on bereft of one who was dearer than life. For those who must bear the death of some loved one, the Catholic doctrine of the communion of saints is the greatest consolation. Death is not annihilation. If the loved one is in Purgatory, the prayers of those on earth will still help; if the loved one is in Heaven, his prayers to God will avail for the sorrowing one on earth. And as has been remarked previously, the Catholic Church has never said of any individual that he is in Hell.

In Catholic moral theology there are many sins enumerated, and some Catholics have committed a goodly number of them. But there is only one unforgivable sin—final impenitence. And we hope that the worst of sinners had the grace of final penitence.

2. Catholicism in the Exterior Life

Although no hard and fast line can be drawn between the interior and the exterior, or public, life of a Catholic, for practical purposes we may say that anything which does not come under the previous section falls in this one. Hence there will be considered here those fields of action of a Catholic affecting the general welfare in addition to the individual's own well-being. The political, economic, and social conduct of a Catholic is, or should be, colored by his Catholicism.

Catholicism should affect every phase of life. Fortunately the American separation of Church and State does not mean the subjection of the Church, or religion, by the State, its confinement to the sacristy, while political, economic, and social activities are freed from the teachings of religion on all these questions.

It is the American tradition that religion is more than attendance at church on Sunday, and that it has a perfect right to express itself on the morality of business and political acts. Catholicism has always accepted this American tradition. It is catholic (with a small "c") as embracing the whole of life in its scope.

Because an American Catholic lives in a democracy, he has the obligation of voting honestly and intelligently as the occasion arises. He should vote so that there may be a reasonable expression of public opinion. For large numbers of religious minded citizens to refuse this responsibility is to allow professional politicians and venal voters to control elections by default. A Catholic either as leader or as led should never become part of a corrupt political machine. Wherever, as a matter of fact, Catholics have formed such groups, they have to that extent been false to their religion. The ideal is that Catholics should inform themselves on the facts and principles of political issues, and then vote in accordance with their convictions.

Catholics should be wise enough not to be deceived by designing demagogues, too shrewd to become the dupes of professional politicians who happen to be nominal Catholics and try to play upon the Catholic sympathies of their fellow religionists. A Catholic's religion should affect his part in politics in the sense that it makes him upright, just, and honest—in a word, as moral in his public as in his private dealings. But a Catholic should not vote for a particular candidate because he happens to be a Catholic; nor should he vote against a candidate simply because that other candidate belongs to some other Church.

There is no Catholic party in this country, and no solid Catholic vote. Some Catholics are Democrats in their political affiliations, and some are Republicans. In some places, it is true, most Catholics of Irish extraction are Democrats; but then in other places, most Catholics of German extraction are Republicans. That is not due to their religion. As a general thing official Catholic leaders refrain from taking sides on purely political issues. They content themselves with enunciating Catholic principles, and leave to Catholic laymen the judgment that such-and-such a political candidate or measure will apply the principle. Indeed, there are very few political questions on which all good Catholics will have the same political opinion.

Catholics heartily support the American separation of Church and State, as explained in the preface. It is true that the Vatican has concordats with many countries defining the relations between the Catholic Church and those specific nations. But this treaty-making of the Vatican does not keep American Catholics from giving their sincere adherence to the situation in the United States where there is no concordat.

For in America we have a tradition which guarantees much more surely than can a treaty with an autocratic government the rights of the American Catholic. And in America the Church has more freedom without union with the State than she enjoys in some countries where she is united with the State. For human nature being what it is, a Church cannot occupy an official civic position without politicians attempting to control it for their own ends—and sometimes politicians are successful in such attempts.

Although Catholics believe that the Catholic Church was founded by Christ, the Incarnate Son of God, has all the truth which He revealed, and is divinely protected from teaching religious error; yet they can also believe that as God tolerates the affiliation of creatures with many different religions, so the State in America should tolerate this condition.[1] It is historically true, of course, that Catholics in Europe at times have persecuted those who did not externally conform to the Catholic Church. But there is nothing in Catholicism to prevent an American Catholic from being loyal to the American principle of freedom of religion—stemming from that good Catholic,

[1] "To imitate God, who, as St. Thomas teaches in allowing evil to exist, 'neither wills evil to be done, nor wills it not to be done, but wills only to permit it to be done; and this is good.'" Encyc. of Leo XIII, "*Libertas, praestantissimum.*"

Cecil Calvert, who established Maryland on this basis. A citizen can be both a good Catholic and a good American. In fact, while not condemning the union of Church and State in other countries, American Catholics may well rejoice in the situation they enjoy here of a fair field and no favor to any one religion.

Sometimes those who admit that Catholics are good Americans now suggest that this is because Catholics are in a minority. Let Catholicism once become the religion of the great majority, they say, and it will be a different story. Then Catholics, so runs the objection, will try to secure special favors for themselves and to place civil disabilities upon others.

Naturally, one cannot predict with any certainty how a group will act a few centuries hence under very different circumstances from the present. If one were inclined to such phophesying, the history of the last twenty years in Germany should surely be a warning. For who in 1918 suspected that the most scientific nation in the world, because of its foolish credulity in unscientific racism, would soon banish its greatest scientists?

But one can say definitely that nothing in Catholicism requires that a Catholic majority should abandon the American principles of separation of Church and State and religious freedom. At the same time, it should be pointed out that there is, humanly speaking, no probability of Catholics, in any near future, becoming a majority in the United States.

The only practical problem is the relation between Catholics as a minority and their fellow citizens as a majority, and a few words may be said on the chief questions confronting them. As citizens Catholics have to take an attitude on the question of war in the abstract and at times also in the concrete. The Catholic position on war in the abstract is: [1] A war can be just or unjust. If a particular war be just, every citizen should respond to the call of his government; and no citizen should participate directly in a war that is unjust.

The conditions for a just war are: 1) it must be in vindication of a violated right; 2) all peaceful means for securing redress must have been exhausted; 3) there must be a prudent judgment that the good accomplished by the war will outweigh the evil; 4) and the means used in prosecuting the war should not in themselves be evil, for a good end cannot justify evil means.

Whether or not these conditions are fulfilled in any concrete circumstances the Church does not, ordinarily, presume to say, but leaves the judgment to the individual's conscience. If any individual is convinced that a war is unjust, he should take no part in it.

Unfortunately, however, under modern conditions, the individual is hardly ever in a position to form a prudent judgment, because he cannot arrive at the facts of the case. He is fed only the information his government wants him to get, he is surrounded by such an atmosphere of propaganda that he is almost bound to think as his government wants him to think.

On the other hand, a Catholic, consistently with the Catholic position on war and in spite of the propaganda and emotional hysteria around him, may hold that a modern war will always result in more evil than good, and, consequently, that a modern war is never justifiable. If the individual Catholic is of this opinion, then he should follow his conscience, no matter what the consequences to himself. He should be a conscientious objector even though that position leads to a concentration camp.

[1] Cf. *"The Church and War,"* by Franziskus Stratman, O.P., N.Y., 1928.

At the same time, the Church does everything she can to lead nations to a wiser way than war of settling international disputes. Every Catholic should do what he can towards the same end. Without being technically pacifist, they should regard peace as one of the greatest blessings a nation can enjoy.

Another important problem is education. Necessarily a Catholic's external life embraces some relations with others in regard to education. As a citizen he cannot escape taxes in support of the State schools, and as a parent he may have to decide whether to send his children to Catholic schools, non-Catholic private schools, or the State schools. About fifty per cent of the Catholics of grammar and high school age are in Catholic schools, and a smaller percentage of Catholic college age students are in Catholic colleges.

The teaching of religion is an all-important matter for the devout Catholic parent. Before school age Catholics should have begun the teaching of Catholicism to their children. It is possible for some homes to teach all of Catholicism that the lay Catholic needs, and the home is still the most important factor in training Catholics. For it is largely in the home that the character of children, for good or ill, is formed. And the living of Catholicism depends upon character. In the ideal home, the child will have been taught, even before school age, to be truthful, honest, obedient, prayerful, and a willingness to undergo some pain or temporal loss rather than fail to obey God's will.

But facing things as they are, it must be admitted that many homes are unable to give their children the systematic knowledge of and training in Catholicism which an adult needs in the world today. Hence Catholics at considerable expense to themselves have built up a system of schools in which Catholicism is taught.

This self-sacrifice on the part of Catholics in supporting two school systems implies no opposition to the underlying fact of the State having its own schools. But Catholics do have the conviction that for the best interests of the State religion should have a place in education. And they hope that some day a way will be found by which, without violating the American principle of separation of Church and State, the religion of the parents will be taught the pupils of State schools. Although a complete solution of this problem of religious instruction may be far in the future, some promising experiments have been undertaken in various parts of the country.

Others besides Catholics are not entirely satisfied with the elimination of religion from the State schools. Thus Dr. F. Ernest Johnson, of Teachers College, Columbia University, writes in his book "The Church and Society," (N.Y., 1935): "Virtually all the religious community would be glad to have some religious teaching in the schools if sectarian controversy could be avoided. Deep in their hearts Protestants do not like secularism in education any better than Catholics do. Experience has taught its lesson. No other way has been found to develop religious concern and loyalty than through education, and the church school, and even 'week-day religious education' have proved to be pitifully inadequate. I am not prepared to propose a remedy, but I am ready to say that it is a badge of mutual ineptitude that Protestants, Catholics and Jews should have found no way to combat the common foe, antisocial secularism, except to remove from our most influential institution for character building the resources for spiritual living that we hold in common" (p. 125).

As remarked above, some persons are worried over what Catholics, now less than seventeen per cent of the population, would do if they increased to a large majority. But a much more practical and pressing question is this: If the present forty-five per cent of the population which is unchurched, and to a large extent unbelieving, becomes an unbelieving seventy-five per cent of the population because its children are getting no religious training in secularized schools, what will it do to the freedom—and especially religious freedom—guaranteed by our Bill of Rights?

Such a majority will not believe in a God to whose moral law the State is subject; it will not believe in a God who grants to each individual citizen the inalienable right to life, liberty, and the pursuit of happiness. Citizens, in the eyes of such an unbelieving majority, will have *no rights,* but only privileges which the State graciously grants and which at its whim it may revoke.

In his justly famous *Commentaries on the Constitution of the United States,* Justice Story remarks: "It yet remains a problem to be solved in human affairs, whether any free government can be permanent, where the public worship of God, and the support of religion, constitute no part of the policy or duty of the state in any assignable shape. The future experiences of Christendom, and chiefly of the American states, must settle this problem, as yet new in the history of the world" (Paragraph 1875).

This was written in 1851, when most schools in America taught religion. Justice Story would probably be even more impressed with the problem of a *free* government enduring when for several generations the great majority of American schools has not taught religion. The man or group devising some workable way for the pupils of the

State schools to be taught the religion of their parents will have done a great patriotic service.

In their civic relations with others, Catholics should wholeheartedly support those movements making for social betterment. Now and then they may seem to hold back because the originators of the movement were not careful enough to plan what was good in itself in a way to allow Catholic participation. But this is the exception, and Catholics should remember that Christ did not hesitate to hold up as an example of brotherly love the Samaritan—although the Samaritan was a heretic from what was then, according to Catholic belief, the true Church of God.

Very rarely in America, if ever, does Catholic belief call for united political action on the part of Catholics. A few years ago, for instance, the moral condition of the movie industry was such that many exemplary persons advocated State censorship. Faced with that situation, Catholics might have thrown their influence with the advocates of political action. But instead, they showed the effectiveness of non-political action. Under the leadership of a committee of bishops they formed what was called "The Legion of Decency," the members of which pledged themselves not to patronize pictures which offended against morals.

On specific pictures there was doubtless sometimes a difference of opinion among Catholics—and also among the non-Catholics who cooperated in "The Legion of Decency." But the general effect, although leaving each individual free to follow his own conscience and attempting no uniformity imposed through civil law, was to raise appreciably the whole moral tone of moving pictures.

Such a method of attacking a moral problem would

seem to be Catholic, American and democratic. It does not insure perfect success. But it may well be more successful than a resort to civil law, and it avoids the irritation and animosity inevitably stirred by one group in a nation using the strong arm of the State to compel the rest of the nation to live up to its standard.

Another example of political inactivity by Catholics is in regard to divorce. Everyone knows that the legislation of the various States, with the exception of South Carolina, allows divorce, and so differs from the teaching of the Catholic Church. But even where Catholics form such a substantial proportion of the population that they, united with others who would agree with them might possibly revise the civil law they have made no effort to do so.

It is true that in a few States local Catholics have tried to prevent the *repeal* of a law preventing the dissemination of contraceptive information. The law in question was passed originally when Catholics were such a minority that they had no influence on its passage. At that time of passage the law represented the conscience of the vast majority of the American people. When it fails to represent the conscience of the majority, it will be repealed. But as Catholics are a part of the American people, and so of its conscience, they have a perfect right to indicate their conscience.

The repeal of a law is on a somewhat different basis from the initiation of a law. And in no case have Catholics used their political power to initiate legislation which would use the civil authority to impose on others the peculiar conscience of Catholics. It may be that in no State are Catholics strong enough to do this; but it may also be that Catholics would not do this no matter how strong they were.

In addition to the political and social spheres represented by the questions so far mentioned, Catholicism has certain principles which should affect the actions of Catholics in the business or economic field. These can be called broadly "social justice," and embrace such principles as a living family wage, the opportunity for everyone to secure a decent living wage by work, the abolition of unemployment.

But just how these principles are to be applied, whether by legislation or organization through non-legislative, and in that sense non-political action; by a revamping of capitalism or by a drastic change of our economic system supplanting capitalism by something else—these remain questions on which Catholics, equally accepting the fundamental principles expounded by Catholicism, differ among themselves. An enunciation of ends is simple, but how to achieve them is extremely complicated, and Catholicism offers no detailed blueprint of how the ends of social justice are to be attained.

Thus Pius XI wrote in his encyclical on atheistic Communism: "Even in the sphere of social-economics, *although the Church has never proposed a definite technical system, since this is not her field,* [this phrase was not italicised in the original] she has nevertheless clearly outlined the guiding principles which, while susceptible of varied concrete applications according to the diversified conditions of times and races and peoples, indicate the safe way of securing the happy progress of society" (# 34).

However, probably most American Catholics are somewhat skeptical of the possibility of achieving social justice through legislation; and many of them fear that one governmental step will lead to another until we have some sort of totalitarian state. But Catholicism leaves the Catholics of various nations free to choose for themselves the means which seem to them best for achieving the ends of social justice. If a particular nation choose fascism, the Church will do its best to get along with fascism. The Church will not take the position that they had no right to make such a choice—provided that their choice does not imply a kind of State inconsistent with their duties to God.

Since God gave man his peculiar nature by which some government is necessary, whatever authority a particular government has comes ultimately from God, but proximately from the people of a nation choosing a particular kind of government, democratic (the rule of the people), or monarchical (the rule of one), for themselves. Every government, whether democratic or monarchical, as the Declaration of Independence said, exists for the good of the governed, and when it ceases to secure that good its title to existence ceases. There is no such thing as the divine right of kings to govern, even though a belief in it profoundly affected history for many centuries. Nor has any individual of any other name a divine right to exercise governmental authority apart from the good of the people.

The Catholic Church exists in every part of the world and its history goes back nearly two thousand years. During that time it has co-existed with many kinds of States, and because of its world-wide extent its adherents have been members of many kinds of States simultaneously. That is, some Catholics have been members of democracies at the same time that other Catholics have been members of monarchies. The Church does not presume to say that one particular kind of State will always and everywhere be best for the good of the people. And utterances of the Pope on the State and governmental authority will be so broad that Catholics under either a monarchy or a democracy can accept them.[1]

Because of this tolerant attitude of the Church, however, towards the people who have chosen some form of monarchical government, it is as illogical to accuse the Church of being out of sympathy with democracy, as to say that it is out of sympathy with monarchism because it does not insist upon Catholics in a democracy using their voting power to change their form of government to that of a monarchy.

At the same time Catholicism teaches certain broad principles which apply to all governments, and which, incidentally, a democracy as well as a monarchy can violate. The first of these principles is that citizens have received from God by the very fact of being men certain inalienable rights admirably expressed in the Declaration of Independence. A second principle might be formulated: a State is bound by God's moral law in its dealings with other States and with its own citizens.

Hence no State is absolutely supreme or the source of all rights. When any State undertakes to regiment the *whole* life of its citizens, to make the citizens exist for the State rather than the State for the citizens, to claim that citizens have no rights except what the State grants—such

[1] An excellent, perhaps the best, treatment of the relations between Church and State is Cardinal Newman's "*Letter to the Duke of Norfolk.*" Anyone who reads that work of several hundred pages will see that no essential incompatibility exists between the teaching of the Catholic Church and a democracy. Seeming difficulties arise from the failure of some critics to interpret certain papal utterances in the logical way in which they were intended. Thus in the so-called Syllabus of Pius IX the proposition was condemned: "Church and State should be separated." But by the condemnation only the contradictory proposition was asserted, and contradictories differ in both quantity and quality. Hence, as the condemned proposition is universal and positive, the proposition affirmed by the condemnation will be particular and negative: sometime somewhere (for instance, in Vatican City or the theocratic State of Solomon) Church and State should not be separated.

a State is exceeding the authority which God has given it and is in conflict with Catholic principles.

Such a totalitarianism is probably more likely to occur in a monarchy (the rule of one, no matter what the specific title), where the actual holder of governmental power has absolutist or regalist conceptions of State authority, than it is in a democracy. But it should be remembered that no *form* of government, *merely by its form*, is necessarily immune from abuse by those who acknowledge no God above them and no God-given as contrasted with State-given rights. If the members of a majority in a democracy are not restrained by a sense of responsibility to a supreme God, they may be as unjust, as tyrannical, and as totalitarian as any dictator and absolute monarch. Probably when Sparta reached its most socialized condition, though it had a sort of democratic form of government, there was as little respect for the rights of the individual citizen as in any contemporary Grecian state with a king. On the other hand, a dictator can feel that he is only God's steward in exercising government power and respect his subjects as equally children of a common Father.

The only sure and safe defense of the connatural and inalienable rights of the citizens against the State is that the possessors of governmental authority should sincerely acknowledge their subjection to the moral law of God, and be guided by a reasonably religious conscience. Anything which undermines belief in God thus endangers human liberty; and anything which tends to confirm belief in the God of Abraham, Isaac and Jacob strengthens the possession of human liberty.

That is an additional reason to the spiritual one, why the Catholic Church deems it so important for Catholic parents to train their children in Catholicism, and why she has gone to such expense to maintain schools where they will be taught such fundamental religious truths. American Catholics think that this is a supremely patriotic service to the Republic.

Yet it must be acknowledged that some rulers, such as Louis XIV and Napoleon Bonaparte, who professed Catholicism, at least nominally, were careless of the Church's conception of the limitations on State authority. But together with this sorrowful admission must go the contention that the Catholic Church tried to exercise a brake upon their absolutist conceptions. If she failed, or if individual officials of the Church went too far in sanctioning absolutism, Catholics have had to pay abundantly.

An American Catholic looking over history may well feel that there has never been for a like length of time and a like extent of population any other government so suited to the Catholic Church as is that of the United States. And likewise, an American Catholic may be convinced that the fundamentals of Catholicism, albeit they are also the fundamentals of some other religions, are necessary for the perpetuation of that government amidst the dangers of the future.

INDEX

INDEX

PART III

PROTESTANTISM IN CREED AND LIFE

BY WILLIAM ADAMS BROWN

BIBLIOGRAPHY

The Church, Catholic and Protestant, William Adams Brown, New York, 1935.

The Church: Its Worship and Sacraments, C. A. Scott, London, 1927.

The Protestant Church as a Social Institution, H. P. Douglass, New York, 1935.

The Church and Society, F. E. Johnson, New York, 1935.

Beliefs that Matter, William Adams Brown, New York, 1930.

Church Unity Movements in the United States, H. P. Douglass, New York, 1934.

Can Christianity Save Civilization? Walter M. Horton, New York, 1940.

For the Healing of the Nations, H. P. Van Dusen, New York, 1940.

The Second World Conference on Faith and Order, Edited by Leonard Hodgson, London, 1938.

The Church and Its Function in Society, W. A. Visser 'tHooft and J. H. Oldham, Chicago, 1937.

I. INTRODUCTION

1. Where Protestants Agree With Catholics and Wherein They Differ

IN HIS interesting and informing chapters on the Roman Catholic religion as creed and life, Father Ross has an advantage to which neither of the other contributors to this symposium can lay claim. He is dealing with a subject matter with clearly defined limits and in the case of most questions can fall back on the teaching of a universally accepted authority. Neither Rabbi Finkelstein nor myself has so simple a task. In my treatment of contemporary Protestantism, as in his of contemporary Judaism, we must interpret the faith of religious bodies which have no single universally accepted spokesman.

This does not mean that Protestants have no objective standards to which their members owe allegiance. Protestants, like the Jews, share with Catholics the acceptance of a written revelation and like them, recognize that this revelation has been progressively interpreted in the course of history. But they believe that this interpretation takes place through the consensus of many individuals acting under the guidance of the Spirit of God. Catholics alone attribute infallibility to a living spokesman. Other Catholics may interpret Scripture, but not with infallible authority.

It is natural, therefore, that Father Ross should begin

his discussion with a definition of papal authority. It is no less appropriate that the present writer should begin his exposition of the faith of Protestants with a brief statement of the conception of religious authority which is held by Protestants. That conception is expressed most clearly in the first chapter of the *Westminster Confession of Faith,* in which we read:

"The Supreme Judge, by whom all controversies of religion are to be determined, and all decrees of councils, opinions of ancient writers, doctrines of men and private spirits, are to be examined, and in whose sentence we are to rest, can be no other but the Holy Spirit speaking in the Scripture.

The authority of the Holy Scriptures, for which it ought to be believed and obeyed, dependeth not upon the testimony of any man or church, but wholly upon God (who is truth itself), the author thereof; and therefore it is to be received, because it is the Word of God.

The whole counsel of God, concerning all things necessary for his own glory, man's salvation, faith and life, is either expressly set down in Scripture, or by good and necessary consequence may be deduced from Scripture: unto which nothing at any time is to be added, whether by new revelations of the Spirit or traditions of men. Nevertheless we acknowledge the inward illumination of the Spirit of God to be necessary for the saving understanding of such things as are revealed in the Word; and there are some circumstances concerning the worship of God and government of the Church, common to human actions and societies, which are to be ordered by the light of nature and Christian prudence, according to the general rules of the Word, which are always to be observed.

All things in Scripture are not alike plain in themselves, nor alike clear unto all; yet those things which are necessary to be known, believed and observed, for salvation, are so clearly propounded and opened in some place of Scripture or other, that not only the learned, but the unlearned, in a due use of the ordinary means, may attain unto a sufficient understanding of them." [1]

This statement is often interpreted to mean that the final authority for the Protestant is the conscience of the individual. There is a sense in which this is true, but it is true in no other sense than that in which it is true of Roman Catholics also. Father Ross has done his readers a service by pointing out that for Catholics as well as for Protestants the ultimate authority is God's Spirit speaking to the conscience of the individual. The difference consists in what each believes God is saying to him.

Important as is this difference and far-reaching as are its effects, it is possible to over-estimate its significance. The differences within Catholicism are greater and the limitations attached to papal authority are more far-reaching than appear at first sight. In Protestantism, on the other hand, we find a consensus which is no less real because we can point to no single clearcut formulation of it such as we find in the great Catholic creeds.

Roman Catholics distinguish two forms of papal authority—that which belongs to the Pope as teacher, and the disciplinary authority given him by Christ for the government of the Church. Father Ross has reminded us of one limitation of the Pope's authority as teacher, the difference, namely, between that which he possesses when he speaks *ex cathedra,* that is as the head of the universal church on a matter of dogma or morals, and that which he shares with other Catholic teachers who expound the historic doctrines of the Church. In the former case he speaks infallibly and must be believed as a matter of faith. In the second case, while obedience is required of Catholics, it is on practical rather than on dogmatic grounds.

[1] Westminster Confession of Faith, Chap. I, Sec. 10, 4, 6, 7.

This opens up a wide range for individual difference, for the points on which the Pope has spoken infallibly are few and far between.

There are differences in Catholicism not only in the realm of belief but in the field of discipline and in the type of religious experience. The Catholic Orders, for instance, by their relatively independent jurisdiction, cut across the diocesan organization and make it possible for men and women of different gifts and temperaments to cultivate forms of the religious life which differ widely from one another.

In 1917 when the Americans entered the war, it occurred to Father John Burke, one of the Paulist Fathers, that to provide for the needs of war service, the Catholics required a single central organization which could act for all alike. But when he tried to act on this belief he was met on all hands with the assertion that it would be impossible to create such a central agency. Person after person whom he consulted told him that, however desirable his plan might be in ideal, it simply could not be done. Father Burke, however, refused to be discouraged. He traveled from one end of the country to the other in order to gain the needed consents, and it was only after fifty or more such obstacles had been successfully surmounted that the Catholic War Council came into being.

As Catholicism in spite of its outward unity makes room for wide difference of individual habit and conviction, so there is agreement among Protestants far greater than at first blush would appear. It will be my aim in the pages that follow, to describe the nature of this consensus and to point out the ways in which it finds expression.[1] Here

[1] Of what follows it should be said that it is impossible to take account of every variant belief of some of the bodies of Christians, small in membership, which lie on the periphery of Protestantism. Some of

it is necessary only to call attention to certain obvious facts which are the presupposition of the discussion.

First of all, Protestants agree with Catholics in accepting the Bible as the authoritative compendium of Divine revelation, the standard by which all later teaching is to be tested. Protestants differ from Catholics in their view of the extent of the canon and in their interpretation of certain texts.

In the next place Protestants agree in accepting, either explicitly or for substance of doctrine, the creeds of the undivided Church. Even those denominations which in principle reject all "man-made creeds," show by their official teaching that in substance they believe the doctrine that the creeds formulate.

Again, Protestants accept the Sacraments of Baptism and the Lord's Supper as divinely authoritative means of Grace, and acknowledge a ministry charged with the responsibility of administering them. As to the nature and significance of the Sacraments and the nature and credentials of the ministry, they differ both from Roman Catholics and among themselves in ways presently to be explained. But here again the differences are less important than the agreements.

Above all, Protestants share a type of religious experience which expresses itself in common worship. They sing the same hymns. They pray the same prayers. They voice the same aspirations. They witness to the same faith. What that faith is we shall presently consider more in detail.

It is clear then that in any attempt to describe the religious life of Protestants we must distinguish between

what is said will not apply to the Unitarians, who do not conceive of themselves as included in Evangelical Protestantism. The Anglo-Catholics within the Anglican communion, moreover, repudiate the designation Protestant, and do not properly come within the purview of this treatment.

that common core of faith and life which they share with one another and the complicated set of institutions and practices through which that common life finds expression. It will help us to form a just estimate of the differences which meet us in contemporary Protestantism if we recall briefly the historic circumstances to which they owe their origin.

2. How Protestantism Came to Be

The first thing to remember about Protestantism is that it began as a reforming movement within the Church of Rome. The last thing the reformers desired to do was to establish a rival church and it was only when they became convinced that the evils against which they protested could not be corrected within the limits of the existing organization that they left the Church of their birth and set about creating an organization which should carry on, in ways which they believed were more consistent with this purpose, the great commission of their Master.

The evils against which the Reformers protested were of two kinds: those which were the result of what they thought an abuse of the Church's authority; and those which grew out of a different conception of the Church's piety. These contrasts still continue. They mark the difference between Roman Catholicism and Protestantism in all its forms and between them determine the nature of Protestant piety.

Rome, as we have seen, finds its ultimate authority in the Pope; Protestants in the Bible,—but not in the Bible considered as a law book, to which one goes for proof texts. That is a view which has often been held by Protestants. But it was not the view of the Reformers or of the classics in which they have defined their position. The true authority for Protestants, as for Catholics, is God speaking to and through His Church. But this Church, as the Protestant conceives it, consists of all those believing spirits who, trusting in God for their salvation turn back to the Book which God has given them for their guidance for the new light which may yet break forth from the Word of God. Protestantism, I repeat, is a churchly religion; and the Bible is not a substitute for the Church, but the book which tells us what the true Church is like and supplies the inspiration for the transformation of life through which alone that true Church can be realized.

The Reformers affirmed that the way to enter upon the Christian life was through an act of personal trust that altered one's relationship to God. This affirmation was given theological expression in the doctrine of justification by faith.

The doctrine of justification by faith is a way of saying in technical language what Jesus said much more simply when he talked about the childlike spirit. It is the Protestant's way of affirming two things about the Christian life which together give it its distinctive quality: first, that it is so wonderful and divine that man can do nothing of himself to earn it, but must be content to take it as a gift; secondly, that it is so adapted to man's true nature that to enter upon it he requires no supernatural change of nature, but only an act of trust which is itself the Gift of God.

Reformers thought certain Catholic practices superstitious and therefore inconsistent with a truly Christian life, so they turned to the rising national states and found in them guarantors of the liberty of worship for themselves which they believed to be essential to Christ's Church.

There was nothing surprising in this. The view of the State as a divine institution charged by God to maintain order and see to it that the Church is protected in its witness and worship, was part of Catholic doctrine, and was taken over naturally by the Reformers. As to the degree of authority which attached to the State, we find the Reformers differing. In some countries, as for example in Germany and England, we find the State given large authority over the Church. In Calvin's Geneva on the other hand and in the Scotland of John Knox, the rising Protestant churches rivalled Rome in their theocratic claim. Whether under establishment or theocracy, it seemed as inconceivable to Protestants as to Catholics that there should be more than one church in one country, and those who dissented from the established regime were regarded as sectarians in the literal sense of the word.

Two new influences must be noted that account for the changed situation which we see today. First, the logic of the actual existence in the community of a variety of religious groups, reinforced by the growing spirit of tolerance which began with the Renaissance and was stimulated by the rise of modern science, made men willing to accommodate themselves to the presence of different forms of religion within the same geographic area. Secondly, the adventurous spirit that sent explorers to the new world, which the voyagers of the fifteenth century had added to the map, led inevitably to a wide diffusion of different types of religion. These adventurers brought with them the religion in which they had been brought up at home. Dissenters came to gain freedom to practice their religion which had been denied them at home; representatives of established churches, to widen the range of their Church's authority. So the divisions which the Old World knew were perpetuated in the New and in due time were succeeded by others of native origin. Nowhere were there to be found within an area of similar size so many different kinds of Protestants as in Colonial America.

Thus there grew up on the new continent a new nation peopled by men of many races and of many nationalities, and to each his own brand of Protestantism was dear. There was not only a Lutheran Church in America, but a German Lutheran Church, and a Swedish and a Norwegian. There was not only a Reformed Church, but a Dutch Reformed Church and a German Reformed Church, and each particular Lutheran or member of the Reformed Church held loyalty to the faith in which he had been brought up a sacred duty.

Side by side with these external changes which brought together on a single continent representatives of so many different types of Protestant Christianity, a second influence was at work even more far reaching in its effects. This was the tolerant spirit which had challenged the prevailing ideal of uniformity and substituted for the conception of a single type of thought and life to which all must conform that of a family of churches each with its own type of life and doctine, yet each recognizing the right of the others to a place with itself in the one all-embracing Church, while all owed civil allegiance to the one nation.

Under the influence of these new conditions, intellectual and practical, we find the attitude of the different Protestant bodies insensibly altering. At first rivals, often jealous rivals, the Protestants of America have come at last to recognize their common heritage as Christians and grant to others (as their fellow-Christians in Britain and on the Continent are beginning to do) the same privileges which they claim for themselves. So that characteristic phenomenon we call a denomination has come to birth in Protestantism, a body having all the characteristics and accepting all the responsibilities of the Church as a whole, yet existing side by side with other similar bodies within the same territory without any official determination of the relation which each should hold to the others.

3. The Types of Contemporary Protestantism

It would not be strange if a Catholic, contemplating all these forms of Protestant religion, should reach the conclusion, which is indeed drawn by many, that it is unscientific to speak of such a thing as Protestantism at all. What really confronts us in contemporary Protestantism, he would be tempted to conclude, is an example of religious individualism run riot. It is important to be reminded, therefore, that the different forms of Protestantism which meet us in history have not grown up arbitrarily but fall into three or four contrasted types with easily distinguishable characteristics.

There is in the first place the contrast between the Lutheran and the Calvinistic, or Reformed type of Protestantism. Lutheran piety has been on the whole of the quietistic sort, content to limit the Church's responsibility to that of witness to God's revelation once for all delivered. Whether it was that Luther, in spite of his leaving the cloister, carried with him some traces of the monastic ideal, or whether there is in the Germanic peoples among whom Lutheranism has found its chief home a quality of inwardness which the Anglo-Saxon lacks, the fact remains that Lutheran piety has been on the whole of an introspective rather than of an active type. More otherworldly than Calvinism, more ready to find its satisfaction within, it has been content to leave the regulation of outward matters to the State and to reserve for the Church the preaching of the Word and the administration of the Sacraments.

Calvinism on the other hand, wherever we find it, in Germany, in France, in Scotland, in Holland, and in the new lands across the sea, has been of a more active type. It has served not only as inspirer of the individual, but as critic of the State. When kings have done wrong and parliaments have gone astray, there has been some Presbyterian preacher to remind them of the fact and to repeat in language appropriate to the historic situation the messages of Amos and Micah. Nor have the Calvinistic churches been content with words. They have followed what they have said with appropriate action. If they have had no bishops, they have had presbyteries; and every pastor has been conscious that in a very literal sense he was a minister by divine authority. So in the Calvinistic churches the disciplinary function of the Church has been revived and the ideal of a Church whose members should be holy has been held aloft.

Anglicanism has qualities in common with both types, as indeed we should expect from its history. In its liturgy it has been the guardian of the Sacramental tradition; in its doctrine it has been prevailingly Calvinistic.[1] More tolerant and comprehensive in its practice than either Lutheranism or Calvinism, it has aspired to be, and at

[1] At least during its earlier period. It is an interesting fact, often forgotten today, that the most uncompromising statement of the doctrine of double predestination, the Lambeth Articles of 1595, was composed by an Anglican Archbishop, Whitgift, and was only prevented from becoming the law of the Church of England by the veto of Queen Elizabeth. Later, like other Calvinistic bodies, the Church of England developed Arminian tendencies, until today we find Anglicans like the present Bishop of Gloucester, who tell us that the Englishman is by nature a semi-pelagian.

times has succeeded in becoming, the church of the nation. Yet it has achieved its comprehensiveness at a price, the price of the unity and consistency which characterizes both the Lutheran and the Calvinistic types. In the Anglican Church, and the Anglican Church alone, men who are genuinely Protestant and men who conceive themselves to be consistently Catholic have been able to find a home side by side.

Different from all three, not only in its form of government but in the quality of its religious life, is the group which constitutes the left wing of Protestantism—the extreme Independents of the Congregational and Baptist types. Here and here alone, we find Protestants who may with some plausibility be called individualists; for here alone we find the doctrine of the universal priesthood of believers carried to its logical consequence. To Protestants of this type the Church is a purely spiritual society, composed of redeemed individuals; and the form of organization they may adopt, or indeed whether they shall adopt any at all, is purely a matter of convenience or efficiency.

Even here, however, there are limits to the individualistic principle and in the existence of the local congregation, with its ministry of the Word and Sacraments, we have a point of contact with other Protestants whose conception of the Church is Presbyterian or Episcopalian. Indeed it may be said that the Congregationalists, just because of the importance they give to individual faith, find it easier to realize the unity of the Church across all ecclesiastical barriers than do members of the more highly organized churches.

In the course of the later history other types have developed which differ in definite respects from all of these and, within the older bodies, new cleavages have appeared. Some of these owe their origin to accidents of history, like a persecution or a migration; others to a difference in Biblical interpretation; still others to the influence of some forceful personality. Such a group are the Baptists who early separated from the other Independents because of their view of baptism as the symbol and seal of conversion. Such a group are the Methodists, who, beginning as a reforming movement in the Church of England, have now become a separate denomination, or rather family of denominations numbering many million members. Such a group are the Quakers, who carry their emphasis upon the spiritual character of the Church so far as to be suspicious of all outward forms of organization and in an age where the individual finds it increasingly difficult to resist the pressure for conformity, remain as a perpetual reminder of the simplicity of primitive Christianity.

With so much of preface we turn to our specific task which is to describe the type of religious faith and life which is common to the great majority of Protestants and which makes them, in spite of all differences, members of the same religious family. We shall consider first the religious convictions which form the creed of Protestants; then the type of life they live whether as individual believers in their personal relation to God, or in their corporate capacity as citizens and churchmen. Finally, a word as to the place of Protestantism in the Church Universal and its possible contribution to the development of an ecumenical Christianity.

II. THE FAITH OF PROTESTANTS

1. What Protestants Believe About God

WE HAVE seen that Protestants agree with Roman Catholics not only in accepting the Bible as an inspired book, the authoritative rule of faith and practice, but also in finding in the Apostles and Nicene Creeds, which are the common inheritance of all Christians, an authentic statement of their faith. Some denominations (e.g., the Anglican and the Lutheran), state this explicitly. Others embody the substance of the teaching of these Creeds in their own formularies. Even those Protestants of the left, like the Baptists, who reject all "man-made creeds" are in the great majority of cases Trinitarians in faith and accept the doctrine of the ancient Creeds as their own.

The extent of this agreement has recently received impressive demonstration. At the Edinburgh Conference of 1937, which brought together for the discussion of questions of faith and order representatives of more than one hundred [1] different ecclesiastical bodies (Orthodox, Old Catholic, Anglican, Lutheran, Presbyterian, Reformed, Methodist, Disciples, Congregationalist, Baptist and Friends), the delegates united in a common affirmation of faith in the "Lord Jesus Christ, the incarnate Word of God" and in "allegiance to Him as Head of the Church and as King of Kings and Lord of Lords."

[1] The exact figure was 122.

An even more impressive expression of the consensus of Protestant belief is to be found in the statement of God's purpose for the World which was unanimously adopted by the Lausanne Conference on Faith and Order in 1927. That statement is as follows:

"The message of the Church to the world is and must always remain the Gospel of Jesus Christ.

The Gospel is the joyful message of redemption, both here and hereafter, the gift of God to sinful man in Jesus Christ.

The world was prepared for the coming of Christ through the activities of God's Spirit in all humanity, but especially in His revelation as given in the Old Testament; and in the fulness of time the eternal Word of God became incarnate, and was made man, Jesus Christ, the Son of God, and the Son of Man, full of grace and truth.

Through His life and teaching, His call to repentance, His proclamation of the coming of the Kingdom of God and of judgment, His suffering and death, His resurrection and exaltation to the right hand of the Father, and by the mission of the Holy Spirit, He has brought to us forgiveness of sins, and has revealed the fulness of the living God, and His boundless love toward us. By the appeal of that Love, shown in its completeness on the Cross, He summons us to the new life of faith, self-sacrifice, and devotion to His service and the service of men.

Jesus Christ, as the crucified and the living One, as Saviour and Lord, is also the center of the world-wide Gospel of the Apostles and the Church. Because He Himself is the Gospel, the Gospel is the message of the Church to the world. It is more than a philosophical theory; more than a theological system; more than a programme for material betterment. The Gospel is rather the gift of a new world from God to this old world of sin and death, the revelation of eternal life in Him who has knit together the whole family in heaven and on earth in the communion of saints, united in the fellowship of service, of prayer and of praise.

The Gospel is the prophetic call to sinful man to turn to God, the joyful tidings of justification and of sanctification to those who believe in Christ. It is the comfort of those who suffer; to those who are bound, it is the assurance of the glorious liberty of the sons of God. The Gospel brings peace and joy to the heart, and produces in men self-denial, readiness for brotherly service, and compassionate love. It offers the supreme goal for the aspirations of youth, strength to the toiler, rest to the weary, and the crown of life to the martyr.

The Gospel is the sure source of power for social regeneration. It proclaims the only way by which humanity can escape from those class and race hatreds which devastate society at present into the enjoyment of national well-being and international friendship and peace. It is also a gracious invitation to the non-Christian world, East and West, to enter into the joy of the living Lord.

Sympathizing with the anguish of our generation, with its longing for intellectual sincerity, social justice and spiritual inspiration, the Church in the eternal Gospel meets the needs and fulfills the God-given aspirations of the modern world. Consequently, as in the past so also in the present, the Gospel is the only way of salvation. Thus, through His Church, the living Christ still says to men 'Come unto me! . . . He that followeth Me shall not walk in darkness, but shall have the light of life.' "

There is much, therefore, in Father Ross' exposition of the Catholic Creed which Protestants can make their own. With him, they recognize that "God is infinite, possessing all perfection in infinite degree," that He is "all good and infinitely benevolent," that "He is the one ultimate reality, eternal and unchanging upon Whom all that is depends and who as Creator has brought the world into being and sustains it in existence and Who has created man in His own image for fellowship with Himself."

With their Catholic fellow-Christians, Protestants recognize that God is Triune and confess Him in the words of the ancient Creed as "Father, Son and Holy Spirit." With them, they believe that God reveals Himself in nature, in history and in the soul of man; but above all, through His Son Jesus Christ, the second person of the Trinity who for us men and for our salvation became man, being conceived by the Holy Ghost, born of the Virgin Mary, was crucified under Pontius Pilate, rose again from the dead on the third day, manifested Himself to His disciples after His death as their living Lord and will come again with glory to vindicate His authority and establish His Kingdom.

Like their Catholic fellow-Christians again, Protestants recognize that there are intellectual difficulties in connection with this belief and that it has often been held in such a way as to contradict the plain teachings of science. They are glad to find, therefore, that Father Ross recognizes that in the past Catholic theologians have sometimes misinterpreted the teachings of the Bible on subjects which fall within the purview of science, and that the Church is ready to acknowledge that theologians have at times made mistakes. Protestants on their part have been guilty of similar mistakes and have their own sins to atone for. In this matter of the adjustment of the claims of faith to the findings of science, Protestants and Catholics face a common problem and it is a satisfaction to know that in many fields of scholarship their representatives are working side by side to mutual advantage.

2. How Protestantism Conceives the Relation of God and Man

It is one thing to accept a creed; another to draw the consequences that follow for life. When we ask how Protestants conceive God's relation to man in detail, we find differences from the view taken by Roman Catholics of far-reaching significance. These differences center about the two points on which the Reformers originally broke with Rome; the nature of the Christian life and the agencies by which it is mediated.

Luther was a monk and, as he himself tells us, one who took the monastic discipline seriously. It was concern for his soul's salvation which had led him to abandon the world for the cloister and that concern made him meticulous in the fulfillment of all his appointed duties. "If ever a monk could have been saved by his monkery," he tells us, "that monk was I." But the penances he practised and the austerities he underwent brought him no peace. On the contrary they made him the more conscious of the imperfection within. Like St. Paul he found two men within him struggling for the mastery, and do what he would the baser had the upper hand.

Then it was that to Luther there came the conviction that he was on the wrong track. It was through a word of the Apostle Paul that the insight came: "The just shall live by faith." Luther perceived that all his striving availed him nothing. He was sure that there was another way, a simpler way: the way of trust which Paul's words pointed out to him; the way of which Jesus, as he understood Jesus, had spoken, the way of the child that does not earn or deserve, but simply receives and is thankful.

With this conviction of Luther we reach that which is distinctive in Protestant piety, the experience of a relation to God which is antecedent to and independent of all merit, a relation which makes direct contact possible and so renders all churchly mediation superfluous.

We may illustrate the Protestant view of the relation of

God to man by contrasting it with two other conceptions of the Christian Life,—the mystical conception of the Christian life as the acquisition of a new divine nature and the legalistic conception of it as the achievement of an adequate degree of merit.

The mystical ideal meets us in more than one of the great Eastern religions, most clearly of all in Buddhism where it is married to a pessimistic philosophy. In Buddhism man wins salvation through the renunciation of desire and achieves his goal in the dreamless sleep of Nirvana. Christian mysticism differs from Buddhist in the central place which it gives to Christ as the divine Being who through His incarnation has deified human nature and made it possible for those who are united to Him by faith to share in His divine and immortal life. In the mystical ideal, whether or not joined with asceticism, the goal is the acquisition of a new immortal nature, in which man shall be rid once and for all of his finiteness and mortality. The mystic believes in the possibility of immediate contact with the divine either through an act of intuition in prayer or through participation in the sacraments, to which in his goodness God has attached a certain mysterious yet life-giving quality.

The Protestant asserts that man needs no change of nature, but only a change of relation. Man is by nature finite, and the finite is incapable of becoming infinite. But man, though finite, need not remain apart from God, since God by His grace has opened a way to Himself by forgiveness. It is sin, and sin alone, that stands between man and his Maker. But God, who is love, has provided a way of escape for man by the sacrifice of Christ; and what man alone cannot do for himself, God has done for him. All that man needs to do is to trust and to repent; and through his trust and the assurance of forgiveness which it brings with it, he will find the motive for the new life which will issue in perfect holiness.

As the Protestant conception of the Christian life differs from the mystical conception of that life as the deification of human nature, so it differs from the legalistic conception of it as the acquisition of merit through the performance of good works.

The conception of merit has no place in the Protestant form of religion. God deals with His redeemed not by law, but by grace. Since through Christ's atonement God has provided a salvation sufficient for all, the Reformers taught that there remains no place for human merit, and they swept away all the elaborate machinery of penance and indulgence. One thing only is necessary: to hear God's word and obey. To him who hears and obeys all good things will be added. Such trust, such obedience, God Himself makes possible. They are God's supreme gift to man and, like all God's gifts, need no human authentication. They shine by their own light.

This does not mean that the Christian is under no obligation to do good works, but only that his motive for doing them is altered. He does them not to gain advantage for himself, but to express gratitude to God who has called him to holiness, and desires for him that he should perfectly realize the life of love.

This change in the conception of piety has far-reaching consequences. It puts an end once and for all to the doctrine of a double standard, that of the Commandments and that of the Counsels, as Catholic theologians phrase it. There are not two kinds of life, one lived by the "religious," technically so-called, who for the purpose of cultivating the life of holiness have cut themselves off from the ordinary life of their kind and in monastery or nunnery have given themselves in intensive fashion to the life of prayer; the other lived by the rank and file of Christians who, still in the world, marry, engage in business and play their part in the many-sided life of their time. There are, to be sure, in Protestantism, distinctions of office. There is a ministry set apart by ordination for the preaching of the Gospel and the administration of the sacraments; but, unlike the Catholic Priesthood, this ministry does not form a distinct order. Its members differ in their function only. While differing in gifts, all Christians together form a universal priesthood—the priesthood of those who, having been redeemed by Christ, witness to others of the grace by which their own lives have been transformed.

This general conception of the Christian life affects all the specific doctrines by which that life is described in detail. It affects the doctrine of sin and of salvation, of faith and repentance, of justification and sanctification, of resurrection and immortality. In each case we find beliefs that in many respects parallel those of Catholicism, but in each case there is a difference of interpretation which has far-reaching practical consequences.

If one were to characterize these differences in a single phrase, one would say that it involved a radical simplification of religion. In the course of history the teaching of the New Testament has received at the hands of the great Catholic theologians an elaborate commentary by which distinctions have been introduced which Protestants do not find there. Thus, more and more, the interpretation of doctrine has become an affair of the specialist and direct access to the Scripture has been made difficult for the ordinary believer. Protestantism reaffirmed his right to this access. It insisted that in spite of the difficulties which the Bible presents, "those things which are necessary to be known, believed and observed for salvation, are so clearly propounded and opened in some place of Scripture or other, that not only the learned but the unlearned in a due use of the ordinary means may attain unto a sufficient understanding of them." [1]

We may illustrate this simplification by the view taken of sin. Protestants agree with Catholics that all men are sinners and that sin consists in any transgression of the righteous will of God. Both agree that sin is of two kinds: original sin which is man's inheritance from his first parents and affects human nature as a whole, and actual sin which consists in the voluntary choice of wrong by the individual. But Catholic theology goes further than this. Father Ross reminds us that in the field of personal choice his Church distinguishes degrees of sin. Some sins are mortal, involving, unless repented of, "a complete loss of man's last end—the beatific vision." Others are venial either because "they involve only a slight digression from the right order" or because "though in themselves a complete turning away from God, they are not such for the agent because of his insufficient knowledge or insufficient consent of the will."

Catholics have built up an elaborate theory in which a distinction is made between the spiritual effect of sin in loss of the divine favor and its temporal consequence in suffering either in this life or in the life to come. Only God can deal with the first on the basis of repentance, but He has authorized His Church to deal with the second through the penitential discipline.

Protestantism does not recognize the distinction between venial and mortal sin.[2] "Every sin, both original

[1] Westminster Confession I, 7.

[2] Westminster Confession of Faith. Chap. 6, Sec. 6.

and actual, being a transgression of the righteous law of God and contrary thereunto, doth, in its own nature, bring guilt upon the sinner, whereby he is bound over to the wrath of God, and curse of the law, and so made subject to death with all miseries spiritual, temporal and eternal." But God, Who is rich in mercy has provided a way of salvation from sin through the atonement of the lord Jesus Christ, Who [2] "by His perfect obedience and sacrifice of Himself, which He through the eternal Spirit once offered up unto God, hath fully satisfied the justice of His Father; and purchased not only reconciliation, but an everlasting inheritance in the Kingdom of Heaven, for all those whom the Father hath given unto Him."

Protestants differ in their view of the way in which the death on the Cross atones for sin and the process through which its benefits are mediated. Some lay chief stress on the penal nature of the atonement as the satisfaction of divine justice; others on its moral influence as leading the sinner to repentance. So they differ as to the exact nature of the divine activity in the process of redemption: some giving first place to the divine choice in election, others to the responsibility of man in accepting or rejecting the divine offer of salvation. But all agree that the atonement of Christ is the one adequate and all-sufficient ground of forgiveness and the assent of the human will in penitence and faith its one indispensable condition.

The way in which man lays hold of the salvation made possible through Jesus Christ is faith. This saving grace which lies at the very heart of the Protestant conception of religion is defined in the Westminster Confession of Faith as due to "the work of the Spirit of Christ in the hearts of the elect. It is ordinarily wrought by the ministry

[2] Westminster Confession of Faith. Chap. VIII, Sec. 5.

of the Word by which also and by the administration of the sacraments and prayer it is increased and strengthened."

"By this faith, a Christian believeth to be true, whatsoever is revealed in the Word, for the authority of God Himself speaking therein, and acteth differently upon that which each particular passage thereof containeth; yielding obedience to the commands, trembling at the threatenings, and embracing the promises of God for this life, and that which is to come. But the principal acts of saving faith are, accepting, receiving and resting upon Christ alone for justification, sanctification, and eternal life, by virtue of the covenant of grace."

"This faith is different in degrees, weak or strong; may be often and many ways assailed and weakened, but gets the victory; growing up in many to the attainment of a full assurance through Christ, who is both the author and finisher of our faith." [1]

Two further aspects of the Protestant view of faith should be emphasized, and may be defined, as follows. First, to the Protestant "the requiring of an implicit faith and an absolute and blind obedience is to destroy liberty of conscience and reason also." [1] Secondly, to the Protestant, good works, while required of the Christian, are the consequence, not the supplement of faith, and so form no basis for the sinner's justification. This depends upon God's free grace alone appropriated by faith. Still less can the good works of others serve in any way as supplement for our own inadequacy and failure.

The obverse of faith is repentance. This is defined in the Westminster Confession of Faith as an evangelical

[1] Westminster Confession of Faith, Chap. XIV, Sec. 1, 2, 3.
[1] Westminster Confession of Faith, Chap. XX, Sec. 2.

grace whereby "a sinner, out of the sight and sense, not only of the danger, but also of the filthiness and odiousness of his sins, as contrary to the holy nature and righteous law of God, and upon the apprehension of His mercy in Christ to such as are penitent, so grieves for and hates his sins, as to turn from them all unto God, purposing and endeavoring to walk with Him in all the ways of His commandments." [2]

Hence, Protestantism requires contrition (perfect sorrow) for the forgiveness of any sin, no matter how slight. In other words, the distinction between contrition and attrition, sorrow that springs from fear, has seemed to Protestant theologians to be without warrant of Scripture and to lead to a lowering of moral standards.

Protestants believe that justification, that is God's acceptance and forgiveness, is antecedent to sanctification and independent of it. It is a gracious act of outgoing love which is made possible by the atonement of Christ and which itself furnishes the motive for the holy life which Protestants, like Catholics, agree is God's will for all men.

At first sight it might seem as if in taking this position Protestants were lowering the moral standard to which the Christian must conform. Surely God, with whom there are no unrealities cannot shut His eyes to the fact of sin or treat one who is in fact a sinner as if he were not. The Protestant believes that it is the genius of love to do this very thing. It is just because God loves man that He does not wait until he has completely reached the goal which God has set for him, but like the Father in the parable, while he is still a great way off, goes out to meet him. Where one is dealing with a difference so great as that between God and man, there can be no such thing as

[2] Westminster Confession of Faith, Chap. XV, Sec. 2.

merit. All that God does for man is beyond his desert, and this fact when apprehended by faith and accompanied by repentance may, and as a matter of fact in the experience of Protestants does, become the supreme motive leading to the victorious moral life.

For it must never be forgotten that for Protestants as well as for Catholics, sanctification in the sense of the conscious quest of the perfect life, is the supreme Christian duty. To say that Protestantism rejects the distinction between Counsels and Commandments and makes no place in its ethics for a special discipline for the making of saints, does not mean that Protestants do not believe in the necessity of the saintly life; only that they regard this as an obligation laid on all believers. It means that Protestants take seriously the word which the Apostle Paul applies to his converts when he speaks of them as those who are called to be saints.

The Protestant view of the nature of the Christian life culminates in the view of its goal. Protestants, Catholics and Jews agree that God has made man an immortal spirit and that the life begun here will continue after death. They agree that man is a composite being consisting of body as well as soul, and they face in common all the difficulties which grow out of this fact. They agree that not only here but in the life after death, man is called to a social life and they confess their faith in the words of the Creed which speak of the "resurrection of the body." Just what this confession means for the Christian in the perplexing new world which has been opened to us by the researches of modern science, it is not easy to say. But of this we can be sure that as for us today the body is the organ through which person communicates his thought to person and joins with others in fellowship and aspiration, so it will be in the life to come. For Protestants as for Catholics, the last scene in the drama of human life is Christ's coming in glory to vindicate His authority and to establish His kingdom. When that time comes the inequalities of life here will be corrected and love and justice alike come to their own.

Nowhere do we find a greater simplification and foreshortening of Christian doctrine than in the view taken by Protestants of the life to come. In every age there has been a minority of Protestants who have taken the prophecy of Christ's physical return to earth literally and believed that in their own lifetime He would come to establish His Kingdom on earth. The great majority, however, have agreed in postponing the final consummation to the end of the ages and in seeing in this present life a preliminary period of discipline and testing. Some Catholics have identified this preliminary period with the Millennium which, following Augustine, they define as Christ's reign on earth through His Church. A few Protestant Creeds point in the same direction. (e.g. Westminster Confession of Faith, Chap. XXV., Section 2.) But the great majority of Protestants reject this view of the Millennium. They therefore postpone the coming of the Kingdom to the last day, or else see in each victory of social justice and humanity which history reveals, a foretaste of its coming.

The sharpest contrast meets us in the conception of the life after death. Catholics interpose between the final stage when there will be only Heaven and Hell an intermediate state called Purgatory, in which all those who have not died in mortal sin will have the opportunity to complete the period of disciplinary suffering which is their due. Protestants recognize only two states for the sinner after death: heaven and hell; although they, too, make place for an intermediate period in which those who have died await the full consummation of the last day. This intermediate period, however, involves no change in moral status. In Protestant teaching, the moral issues of life are finally determined at death. To quote the Westminster Confession of Faith, "the souls of the righteous being then made perfect in holiness, are received into the highest heavens, where they behold the face of God in light and glory, waiting for the full redemption of their bodies; and the souls of the wicked are cast into hell, where they remain in torments and utter darkness, reserved to the judgment of the great day. Besides these two places for souls separated from their bodies, the Scripture acknowledgeth none." [1]

In this account of the formal teaching of Protestants, I have relied for the most part on the statements of the Westminster Confession of Faith, because that is the most complete and final formulation of Protestant doctrine that we possess and because many of its definitions have become classics and would be accepted by other Protestants as well. But any attempt at a comprehensive statement of Protestant doctrine must be subject to two qualifications: First, the differences (of emphasis, if not of formal teaching) which result from the presence within Protestantism of the contrasting types of thought and life already referred to; and secondly, the changed interpretation of the older doctrines made necessary by the new light which modern science has shed both on the nature of the biblical revelation and on that other book of God, whose authority both Catholics and Protestants recognize, the book of Nature.

Examples of the first type of variation are the differing views taken of the relation between predestination and

[1] Westminster Confession of Faith, Chapter XXXII, Section 1.

free will and of the nature and effect of the Atonement. Examples of the second are the changes brought about in the view of creation and of the primitive state which result from the widespread acceptance of evolutionary theory.

Calvinists have, for the most part, held a high doctrine of predestination and have accepted its corollary in the decree of double election. Arminians on the other hand, set no limit to the Grace of God, but that which man sets for himself by his own choice. So we find a contrast between those who hold a doctrine of limited atonement in the sense that though Christ's sacrifice is sufficient to atone for all, it is limited in God's purpose to the elect, and those who hold that this purpose is all-embracing, and on that fact base their hope of the possibility of the final salvation of all. In general, it may be said that in recent years the more rigid views of the older Calvinism have been modified or abandoned. There is general recognition that in this matter of predestination and free-will we are dealing with a mystery to which our human logic can supply no definite solution. The prevailing opinion among Protestants today is well expressed in the report of Commission I of the Edinburgh Conference of Faith and Order, on the meaning of Grace.

"In regard to the relation of God's grace and man's freedom," this report declared, "we all agree simply upon the basis of Holy Scripture and Christian experience that the Sovereignty of God is supreme. By the Sovereignty of God we mean His all-controlling, all-embracing will and purpose revealed in Jesus Christ for each man and for all mankind. And we wish further to insist that this eternal purpose is the expression of God's own loving and holy nature. Thus we men owe our whole salvation to His gracious will. But, on the other hand, it is the will of God that His grace should be actively appropriated by man's own will and that for such decision man should remain responsible.

"Many theologians have made attempts on philosophic lines to reconcile the apparent antithesis of God's sovereignty and man's responsibility but such theories are not part of the Christian faith.

"We are glad to report that in this difficult matter we have been able to speak with a united voice so that we have found that here there ought to be no ground for maintaining any division between Churches."

The widest departure from the views of the older Protestantism has taken place in the view of creation and of the primitive state. Here the researches of modern science have made it increasingly difficult to hold the older view of creation, as having taken place in six days of twenty-four hours. Both Catholic and Protestant scholars find nothing in their theology which is inconsistent with the acceptance of the evolutionary hypothesis. So, many Protestants regard the story of the fall in the first chapter of Genesis as a parable in which eternal truth concerning the nature and consequences of sin is set forth in poetical language.

3. The Protestant View of the Nature and Function of the Church

From our study of the Protestant view of the nature of the Christian life, we turn to the agencies by which it is mediated. This leads us to consider the Protestant conception of the nature and function of the Church.

The first thing that strikes a Protestant when he enters a Catholic Church is the extremely concrete way in which

Catholic piety finds expression. It is mediated by physical objects: Statues of saints, pictures of the Virgin and of the Christ child, the crucifix, not to speak of a host of lesser and more personal objects like the rosary and the scapular, fix the attention of the worshipper and give definiteness to his meditation. There are in some Roman Catholic Churches not one altar but many, and each has its relic commemorating the virtues and the sacrifice of some particular saint. There are holy actions too, like the elevation of the Host or the sign of the Cross. There are holy places, like the Grotto of Our Lady of Lourdes or the shrines that commemorate episodes in the life of the Saviour or of some later saint. Above all there are holy persons, officially canonized by the Church. Catholic religion is accessible religion. Through its symbols—and they are everywhere—it brings God near to the worshipper. It reminds him that there is another world than that of business and pleasure in which most of our working hours are spent. It invites him to fellowship with the eternal.

By contrast, Protestant worship seems to the Catholic to be formal and bare. The pulpit takes the place of the altar. The minister is first of all preacher and only incidentally priest. And while the sacraments have their place they are celebrated seldom and without the elaborate pomp and ceremony with which the Catholic Church surrounds them.

This more formal character of Protestant worship is a natural result of its history as a reforming movement. From the first, Protestantism has appealed to the intelligence of its worshippers. The minister is not there to tell his congregation what they do not know; rather to remind them of those simple but essential truths which God has made known to His children through the Bible: truths equally accessible to each worshipper if he will study God's revelation for himself.

Protestantism began, therefore, as a religion for laymen and that has remained its characteristic ever since. The first dogmatic treatise of Protestantism, Melancthon's *Loci,* was a brief compendium of doctrine dealing with those truths of Scripture which were essential for salvation and which each sincere reader, if he approached the Bible in humility and prayer, might discover for himself.

This democratic attitude has characterized Protestant religion throughout its history. It determines the Protestant view of the Church as a fellowship of believers united by a common faith and called to a common task. This does not mean that the Protestant thinks of the Church as a group of individuals who have come together to form a society much as Rousseau conceived the origin of political society as a social contract. The very reverse is true. When a man has faith in God (at least as Christianity conceives that faith), he is no longer an isolated individual but by that very act becomes a part of the Christian fellowship, responsible with his fellow Christians for a corporate as well as for an individual life.

This is true of all types of Protestantism, those of Congregational polity as well as Presbyterians and Episcopalians. The Baptist, no less than the Presbyterian and the Episcopalian, is a churchman. Only in his case the basic social unit is the local congregation and the Church Universal becomes the fellowship which is composed of the members of all the congregations that have confessed Christ and have consecrated their lives to His service. So strongly indeed do some Baptists emphasize the dependence of the individual upon the congregation for a full Christian life that, unlike some other branches of the

Church, they deny that there can be a valid celebration of the communion except in the presence of the local congregation.

To the Protestant then, the Church is a spiritual society consisting of all those who are joined to Christ by repentance and faith, and who through that faith have discovered their fellowship with one another. Like their Catholic fellow-Christians, and like the Jews, Protestants distinguish between the Church visible and the Church invisible. "The Visible Church consists of all those throughout the world that profess the true religion together with their children. The invisible Church consists of the whole number of the elect who are or shall be gathered into one under Christ, the Head thereof, and is the spouse, the body, the fullness of Him that filleth all in all."[1] The churches we see contain many who are imperfect and who, in God's sight, do not deserve the Christian name. The number who belong to the Church invisible is known to God alone. The Catholic conception of the Church differs from the Protestant conception in that it adds to the spiritual qualities which Catholics and Protestants alike attribute to the Church a sacramental and a legal quality.

To the Catholic, I repeat, the Church is a sacramental institution through contact with which man touches the present supernatural. It is only fitting therefore, that much of Father Ross' exposition of Catholic belief should be taken up with a detailed account of the nature and operation of the Sacraments. These are physical acts in which divine grace is not only symbolized but through which it is imparted.

The Catholic view of sacramental grace explains the

[1] Westminster Confession of Faith, Chapter XXV, Sec. 2 and 1.

unique position of the priesthood in Catholic religion. A priest is a person who by his ordination has received the power to communicate God's grace through certain sacraments as no other Christian not similarly endowed can do. This power is imparted by the laying on of the hands of the bishop, who in his turn stands in the order of apostolic succession.

This conception of the priesthood explains the attitude of the Catholic to intercommunion. Whether he be Orthodox, Roman or Anglican, he believes something is needed for the full efficacy of the sacraments which he misses in the Protestant ministry.

Besides the seven sacraments described by Father Ross, the Catholic recognizes other acts which, while not sacraments in the strict sense, are helps in the Christian life. These sacramentals are of many kinds and each in its own way serves to make God real.

In place of this elaborate system by which the Catholic Church touches man's life at every point, Protestants recognize two external means through which God's grace is mediated and two only: the Word and the sacraments. By the Word, is meant the contents of the Gospel as authoritatively set forth in the Bible and transmitted to succeeding generations by the preaching of the spoken Word. By a sacrament the Protestant understands "a holy sign or seal of the covenant of Christ immediately instituted by God to represent Christ and His benefits and to confirm our interest in Him as also to put a visible difference between those who belong to the Church and the rest of the world, and solemnly to engage them to the service of Christ according to His Word." [1]

Only two such sacraments are regarded by Protestants

[1] Westminster Confession of Faith XXVII, Section 1.

as having scriptural authority: Baptism and the Lord's Supper. "Baptism is a Sacrament of the New Testament, ordained by Jesus Christ, not only for the solemn admission of the party baptised into the visible Church, but also to be unto him a sign and seal of the covenant of grace, of his ingrafting into Christ, of regeneration, of remission of sins, and of his giving up unto God, through Jesus Christ, to walk in newness of life." [1] The Lord's Supper is the "Sacrament of Christ's body and blood, to be observed in His Church unto the end of the world, for the perpetual remembrance of the sacrifice of himself in his death, the sealing all benefits thereof unto true believers, their spiritual nourishment and growth in Him, their further engagement in, and to all duties which they owe unto Him; and to be a bond and pledge of their communion with Him and with each other as members of His mystical body." [2] While it is not a repetition of the sacrifice of Christ, but only a commemoration of it, it is not a mere memory but a means through which "worthy receivers outwardly partaking of the visible elements in this Sacrament, do then also inwardly by faith, really and indeed, yet not carnally and corporally, but spiritually, receive and feed upon Christ crucified, and all benefits of his death: the body and blood of Christ being then not corporally or carnally in, with, or under the bread and wine; yet as really, but spiritually, present to the faith of believers in that ordinance, as the elements themselves are to their outward senses." [3]

But while Protestantism thus limits the range of sacramental religion in the technical sense, this is not to be thought of as a narrowing of the area of the present super-

[1] Westminster Confession of Faith XXVIII, Section 1.
[2] Westminster Confession of Faith XXIX, Section 1.
[3] Westminster Confession of Faith, Chapter XXIX, Section 7.

natural, but rather as a re-emphasis of the spiritual character of God's presence in His world. The true logic of the Protestant position is drawn by the Quakers, who reject all outward sacraments, not because they deny the sacramental principle, but because they believe that in the historic Church, it has been too narrowly restricted. To the faith of the Society of Friends, all life should be sacramental: every washing a baptism; every breaking of bread a Lord's Supper.

This is indeed the ideal of all Protestants, however imperfect may be their approximation of it. While in theory Protestants reject the other five sacraments of Rome, they provide in their practice for the needs which these are designed to meet. Confirmation is a common practice in all the larger Protestant churches. Ministers are set apart for their office by ordination through the laying on of hands. Marriage is celebrated as a religious rite to which many Protestants attribute sacramental significance. Only penance and extreme unction have no definite ecclesiastical parallels in Protestantism and this is due not to any failure to recognize the religious significance which attaches to confession or the comfort which the presence of the minister may bring to the dying but because of a reaction against what Protestants believe to be superstitious practices which have attached to the Catholic interpretation of those rites.

The Protestant holds that confession of sin may and should be made by the sinner directly to God and that such confession is a prerequisite of forgiveness and alone is necessary to secure it. While the confession of "faults one to another" may often be spiritually helpful, it is not essential and there is no need of mediation between God and man save that of the "man Christ Jesus."

Even the Church, in Protestant thought, cannot stand between the soul and God. Protestantism finds in the Scripture no doctrine of priestly mediation that limits the individual's right of immediate access to God. There is no Scriptural authority, therefore, for thinking of the Church as an institution given by God infallible authority to interpret His will or to administer discipline in His name since every soul is directly responsible to God and may commune directly with Him.

The commission given by our Lord to Peter, "Thou art Peter and upon this rock will I build my Church," was, as Protestants understand it, given to Peter not as an individual merely but as confessor. The support that Peter gave to the first stones of the ecclesia is abundantly set forth in the first ten chapters of the Book of Acts. Protestants find no evidence that Peter exercised any authority of a nature capable of transmittal to successors and find the historical evidence of unbroken continuity too uncertain to sustain so weighty a theory as that of Apostolic succession and its spiritual implications. This conviction inevitably affects the Protestant doctrine of the Church.

Protestants find in the history of Protestantism itself evidence that their conception of religion and their efforts to practice it enjoy the favor of God. It is thus that they account for the singular evidences of His grace which have accompanied Protestantism throughout its history. Protestants in general think it reasonable to conclude that God has more than one way of dealing with His children; that if He has provided for those who feel the need of external authority an answer to this need in the Church of Rome, so He has made His presence known to those whose natural way of approach is more direct by the more democratic methods for which Protestantism makes room.

It follows from this general point of view that Protestants do not think of the ministry as a distinct order, either of sacramental gift or of legal jurisdiction; but as that part of the whole family of believers upon whom God has bestowed special gifts of teaching and administration.

In practice, it is of course true, that Protestants like Catholics, make place for law in the administration of the Church and this in two ways. As corporations organized under State law, churches are subject to the laws of the State and must, under all normal conditions, conform to its requirements. But, in addition, each denomination has formulated its own form of government in rules which under ordinary circumstances have for its members the force of law. The difference is that in Protestantism these rules are not part of the essence of the Church. They come under the general principle set forth in the first chapter of the Westminster Confession of Faith, that there are some circumstances concerning the worship of God and the government of the Church, common to human actions and societies, which "are to be ordered by the light of nature and Christian prudence, according to the general rules of the Word which are always to be observed." (Chap. I, Section 6.)

What the writer has thus far tried to describe is the prevailing Protestant view of the Church as it meets us in the larger Protestant denominations. It is only fair to say, however, that in the course of history we find variations from the prevailing type, both in the conservative and in the radical direction. Examples of the first are the *jure divino* theories which from time to time meet us in Protestantism; theories in which some particular form of government, Presbyterian, Episcopalian, Congregational, as the case may be, is identified with biblical teaching. At the other extreme we find a certain type of Congregationalism which carries its emphasis upon the autonomy of the individual so far as to make no real place for any form of organized Christianity. But those are departures from the prevailing type which has in the main, the characteristics above described.

Mention should be made, too, of one type of churchmanship which has played a great role in the early history of Protestantism, from which today we find a widespread and wholesome reaction. I mean the type of Old Testament Christianity known as Puritanism. Characteristic of this view is a negative attitude toward all those aspects of historic Christianity for which no definite warrant can be found in biblical teaching. Especially unfortunate was the attitude taken by the Puritans toward beauty in worship. Many aspects of the historic liturgy which we now recognize as entirely consistent with Protestant principles they rejected and denounced. Fortunately, most Protestants have come to see that this iconoclastic Puritan attitude is no part of authentic Protestantism, and the way is open for them to recover a part of their Catholic inheritance which they have needlessly renounced.

One of the most encouraging aspects of the contemporary situation is the sympathetic attitude taken by many Protestants to the Roman Catholic Church. Whereas they were once content to denounce, they now try to understand. This new spirit of appreciation which we are glad to believe is shared by Catholics in their attitude toward Protestants is full of promise for the future.

4. How Protestants Deal With Differences of Conviction

An impartial observer contemplating the two views of the Church, Catholic and Protestant, here passed in review, will be struck first of all by the contrasts in definiteness. In Catholicism we have a clear cut theory in which each eventuality is foreseen and every problem furnished with its appropriate solution. In Protestantism, on the other hand, everything seems at loose ends. Instead of a single, definite theory to which everything must conform, we have a spirit and way of approach which makes room for wide variation and in which the student is surprised, now and again, by meeting disconnected fragments of the older Catholic inheritance.

This contrast appears most clearly in the differing attitudes taken towards tradition. Catholics and Protestants agree that the Bible, which both accept as authoritative, requires an interpreter. Both alike, face the problems which are presented to anyone who would qualify for this office by the radical changes introduced into our way of thinking by the complicated system of insights and discoveries that we sum up under the name of modern science. But while Catholics meet this problem with a definite technique in which the responsibility for such additions or readjustments as may prove necessary is put upon some recognized authority, Protestants have no theoretical solution of the problem which is involved in the relation of the Bible to tradition. Scripture, we are told in the Westminster Confession of Faith (Chapter I, Section 9), is its own interpreter. "When there is a question about the true and full sense of any Scripture (which is not manifold, but one) it may be searched and known by other places which speak more clearly."

Unfortunately, the application of this principle has not always led to the same results and we find that in the course of history, different interpretations have been held by Protestants and these interpretations, formulated in creeds and Confessions of Faith, have been made the occasion of granting or withholding fellowship.

Thus tradition, banished from the door, has returned by the window. In general, we find two contrasting attitudes in Protestantism: the more conservative, represented in its extreme form by Puritanism, has been suspicious of everything that goes beyond the plain word of Scripture and hence has been critical of the Church's Catholic inheritance; the other more liberal has been inclined to accept as legitimate whatever part of historic Catholicism could not be shown to be definitely disproved by Scripture.

Thus, there was introduced into the heart of Protestantism a fundamental inconsistency, the inconsistency between a theory that affirmed the duty of the individual Christian to think for himself and a practice which denied it. In criticising his Church when it seemed to him to depart from the teaching of the Bible, the individual church member was doing what the creed of his Church told him he ought to do. Yet so long as that Church made church membership dependent upon the holding of a uniform system of doctrine, such criticism presented the church with an insoluble problem. Where exactly was the point at which conformity ceased to be a duty and differing views became admissible within the church? That there was such a range of permissible variation all Protestants admitted. Luther used large liberty in his interpretation of Scripture and more than two centuries later the American Presbyterians, in adopting their form of government in 1788, put on record their conviction that while "they think it necessary to make effectual provision, that all who are admitted as teachers be sound in the faith; they also believe that there are truths and forms, with respect to which men of good characters and principles may differ. And in all these they think it the duty both of private Christians and societies, to exercise mutual forbearance towards each other." [1]

But how was one to tell just which they were? In Catholicism there are ways of determining the limits of admitted difference and of dealing with an offender when he has gone wrong. Protestantism has had no such generally accepted method and for lack of a better alternative has fallen back upon the method of the older church, with its heresy trials and its resulting excommunication.

What is clearly needed then, if Protestantism is to vindicate its claim to represent a distinct type of Christian life and thought, is some general clearing house where the consensus of its beliefs can be determined and exhibited.

This missing link in the organization of Protestantism, the Ecumenical Movement seeks to supply. It would not be fair to describe the Ecumenical Movement as a Protestant Movement, since from the first, Catholics (Eastern Orthodox and Old Catholics) and Protestants have cooperated in it. But it is true that it has afforded Protestants (as for that matter it has afforded the Eastern Orthodox) the opportunity to carry on a systematic study of their agreements and disagreements. In this respect, the World Conferences of Lausanne (1927) and of Edinburgh (1937), deserve the attention of the Church historian as registering significant progress in the realm of doctrinal theology.

The contemporary Protestant view of the relation of

[1] The Constitution of the Presbyterian Church in the United States of America (Philadelphia 1895) Form of Government Chapter I, Preliminary Principles Sec. V, p. 283.

the Bible and tradition, was the subject of discussion by Commission II of the Edinburgh Conference, and its findings on the subject of tradition are summed up in the Conference Report: "By tradition is meant the living stream of the Church's life. Thus the Orthodox East, but not it alone, allows that there may be widespread opinions which, as being contrary to Scripture, cannot be considered to have the true authority of tradition, but it does not exclude from tradition some beliefs which do not rest explicitly on Scripture, though they are not in contradiction with it.

"We are at one in recognizing that the Church, enlightened by the Holy Spirit, has been instrumental in the formation of the Bible. But some of us hold that this implies that the Church under the guidance of the Spirit is entrusted with the authority to explain, interpret and complete the teaching of the Bible, and consider the witness of the Church as given in tradition as equally authoritative with the Bible itself. Others, however, believe that the Church, having recognized the Bible as the indispensable record of the revealed Word of God, is bound exclusively by the Bible as the only rule of faith and practice and, while accepting the relative authority of tradition, would consider it authoritative only in so far as it is founded upon the Bible itself." [1]

The former of these views represents the position of the Eastern Orthodox and Anglo Catholics, the latter of the great majority of Protestants.

More significant than any specific agreement in teaching is the provision made in the Ecumenical Movement for the systematic exploration of the consensus and dissensus of existing churches. By this provision the missing link in

[1] Pages 230 and 231.

Protestant organization has been supplied. The writer's sense of the importance of this provision may be gathered from words spoken by him on the platform of the Edinburgh Conference when the matter of scripture and tradition was under discussion:

"I want to call attention to the fact that we are, in our actual procedure in this Conference, making progress toward dealing with the most difficult and delicate of all the points that separate us, namely the relation of Scripture and tradition. When we consider this matter we are involved in almost insuperable difficulties. When we ask our friends of the Orthodox Church how they are to discover and define for us the nature of the tradition they would associate with Scripture, they find themselves in embarrassment because they have no means of expressing their interpretation of tradition in an orderly and systematic manner. On the other hand, the Reformed Churches, which deny the authority of tradition, have set up creeds and confessions as standards without providing any way of dealing in orderly fashion with the differences which these standards reveal. Through the Ecumenical Movement we are providing the machinery through which we can approach the practical solution of these difficulties in a way that is in keeping with our convictions. By the method of brotherly conversation we are finding it possible to determine that central consensus which has been growing up since Scripture times, and which is common to Protestants and Catholics, and this in a way which has hitherto been impossible since the breaking up of the Church into separate traditions." [1]

Even more significant than its contribution to the defini-

[1] I have somewhat expanded the brief account of these remarks printed in the official minutes.

tion of the consensus of Protestants, is the indication given by this procedure of a new attitude on the part of Protestants toward the Catholic contribution to Christianity. Protestants are no more willing than Catholics to regard themselves as a sectarian form of Christianity. There is nothing that is true in Catholic Christianity which their principles should not lead them to welcome. For this reason, every such friendly discussion between Catholics and Protestants as has given rise to this book is to be welcomed.

III. PROTESTANTISM AS A WAY OF LIFE

1. Protestantism as Ideal and as Experience

FROM the Creed which Protestants profess, we pass to the kind of life they live. Here we meet in accentuated form the contrast between ideal and experience. Father Ross recognizes this contrast in his own exposition. He frankly confesses that not all Catholics live up to the principles of their religion. The Church, he tells us, "is made up of good, bad and indifferent men. She knows that this is so as Christ by several parables said that it would be, and She suffers all to grow until the harvest. It is only in exceptional cases that She excommunicates any individual by name and even then the door for his return is always open."

Very wisely therefore, Father Ross makes no attempt to draw the line between these different kinds of Christians or to evaluate the extent to which, in effect, the principles of the Christian Life are lived up to by Catholics. He is content to draw "a picture, even if an inadequate one," of "how the Catholic who wishes can live Catholicism."

The present writer will follow the example thus set. He will make no attempt to determine how far Protestants realize the ideal set them by their religion. It will be enough if he can point out what that ideal is.

We shall be helped in our understanding of the Protestant ideal by considering how the Protestant understands sainthood.

Among the deathless sentences which Jesus sent ringing down the centuries is one which in its demands upon the capacity of man seems to set a standard which surpasses the human. "Be ye perfect," he is reported once to have said to His disciples, "even as your Father which is in heaven is perfect." [1]

Yet, in every age, there have been men and women who have taken this word of Jesus seriously and have made perfection their goal. We call these heroic spirits saints. In them we see to what heights God's grace may lift the man who puts himself unreservedly at God's disposal. In them, too, man's differing ideals of perfection meet us in sharpest contrast.

The Protestant belief is that only when we see Christ face to face in another world shall we be wholly conformed to His image.

None the less Protestants are committed to the daring doctrine that all Christians are called to be saints. They believe that in conversion the resources which a man possesses for his struggle against sin are augmented and that he is enabled by God's grace to approximate in varying degree the perfect life to which all are called. Yet since Christ has made an atonement sufficient for all, there remains no place or need for the acquisition of further merit from the sacrifices of the saints. In sainthood as the Protestant conceives it the emphasis is on the active life. The saints Protestants most delight to honor are not the mystics, for mysticism tends to draw attention away from the affairs of this passing world to the eternal verities of the world which is unseen. The excellence in which the

[1] Matt: 5:48.

mystic takes supreme delight is beauty—a beauty which transcends all the lesser beauties which are open to us by sense perception. The Protestant saint, on the other hand, is a man of action, and action in the world of affairs. The task set him by God, as he conceives it, is to do God's will in the station to which he has been called. Righteousness is the quality in God of which he is most vividly conscious —a righteousness which finds its clearest expression in God's dealing with moral evil, in the individual and in society.

The primacy given by the Catholic to the contemplative life explains many things about the Catholic saints which repel the average Protestant. It gives a reason for their ascetic practices. These are not valued for themselves but because they help to free the will from its engrossing preoccupations and enable the individual to concentrate attention upon the divine mystery. Money, sex, the right to go one's own way and to live one's own life, whatever might conceivably divert the will from its supreme task, all must be given up. But the great saints have not been content with the surrender of these lesser goods. They have aspired to be rid of selfhood altogether and to become one with God in an ineffable experience, in which not thought or desire merely but consciousness itself disappears.

Protestants on the other hand emphasize the active life. They see God at work in the world of men and feel called to follow Christ in His human ministry of love. This ministry should not require a man to leave the world and enter a cloister; rather to bring to the tasks and problems of every day the singleness of mind and will that will make of all life a ministry, a worship expressing itself in deed. The Protestant believes that every calling may be a priesthood, that all work may be holy, and that scientists and statesmen, housewives and farmers, teachers and bankers are called by God to be His saints as truly as monk or nun.

So the saints of Protestantism are to be found in the world doing their daily tasks, whatever these may be: statesmen like Lincoln, soldiers like Gordon, philanthropists like Shaftesbury, missionaries like Wesley, preachers like Phillips Brooks; but wherever they are found, they are living a life made possible through faith in God.

I am well aware that the matter is not so simple as this. Many of the Catholic saints have lived active lives. They have been scholars, administrators, even husbands and wives, whereas we find in Protestantism many who like William Law have been virtuosi in the life of prayer. Nevertheless if we ask what is characteristic of Catholic piety it is the ascetic life; whereas the Protestant ideal is that of the man or woman who most completely exemplifies the Christian faith in the place to which God, in His providence, has called him.

2. The Genius of Protestant Piety

We turn now to our special theme: the description of the kind of life which a Protestant would live if he realized the ideal set for him by his own religion. We may sum this up in two words. It would be a life of worship and a life of service.

Protestants give first place to the devotional reading of the Bible as the most effective means of cultivating a life of prayer. In public worship Protestants put the sermon in the central place. This is not because they wish to magnify the preacher but because the sermon is the most effective way to bring to the attention of the worshipper the central teaching of the Bible and to draw its consequences for the personal Christian life.

Like Catholic piety, Protestant piety should begin in the home. It finds its characteristic expression in family worship. At no point has Protestantism departed more widely from its original ideal than in the widespread neglect of family prayers. This neglect is all the more serious because Protestants have not ordinarily at their disposal those visible reminders of the claims of their religion which play so large a role in Catholic piety—the Crucifix, the Rosary, pictures and statues of the Saints and of the Virgin, and the like.

In the normal Protestant home, religious training begins early. The child is taught to read the Bible and it may be to learn parts of it by heart. As soon as he is old enough he is taken to Sunday School where he receives systematic instruction in the principles of his religion. Later he accompanies his parents to Church and when he reaches years of discretion becomes a member of a Communicant's Class and after having been examined by bishop, minister or session as the case may be, is admitted to the Communion.

Most Protestants practice infant Baptism, though the Baptists and Disciples of Christ believe that Baptism should be deferred until it can be associated with a conscious profession of faith. In the case of the other communions the child of believing parents is baptised in infancy and is regarded by this act as already in principle a member of the visible church.

With his first communion, the child who has been baptised is initiated into the meaning of sacramental religion. If he is a Presbyterian he may be reminded of the significance of the Sacrament of which he is about to partake by hearing the minister repeat the introductory words of the Book of Common Worship: "Dearly beloved, as we draw near to the Lord's Supper to celebrate the Holy Communion of the Body and Blood of Christ, we are gratefully to remember that our Lord instituted this Sacrament to be observed in His Church unto the end of the world: for the perpetual remembrance of the sacrifice of Himself in His death, the sealing all benefits thereof unto true believers, their spiritual nourishment and growth in Him, their further engagement in and to all duties which they owe unto Him; and to be a bond and pledge of their union with Him and with each other as members of His mystical body." Then follow the words of the institution, the setting apart of the elements by prayer and their distribution to the worshippers. The service concludes by prayer and the singing of a final hymn.

One thing which surprises Catholics in the Protestant attitude towards the Sacrament is the infrequency of its celebration. In most Protestant churches the Lord's Supper is celebrated once a month, sometimes not so often. Only the Episcopalians, who have been most conservative in their attitude toward the older Catholic practice, and the Disciples of Christ who model their worship on New Testament precedents, have preserved the custom of frequent Communion. It is natural to conclude, as indeed many Protestants do, that the Sacrament is a relatively unimportant part of religion.

This is a departure from the genius of original Protestantism. The reason why the Sacrament was celebrated seldom was not that it was believed to be unimportant. On the contrary, it was because it was thought so sacred a part of religion that it was dangerous to approach the Lord's Table without the most careful preparation. Those who intended to communicate were therefore urged to attend a preparatory service during the preceding week, to prepare themselves individually by self-examination and prayer. In many cases (notably in Scotland) they were expected to notify the minister of their intention to be present at the service. One of the most encouraging features in contemporary Protestantism is the growing recognition by Protestants of the importance of the Lord's Supper for the cultivation of the devotional life, the provision for its more frequent celebration and the increasing tendency to regard the practice of intercommunion as the final test of the unity of Christ's Church.

A further mark of the difference between Catholic and Protestant piety is the absence from the latter of the devotion paid to the Virgin and the Saints.

This is due in part to historical reasons. As the Protestant Reformers found no scriptural authority for the central place given to the Pope, so they found no such authority for the unique place given by Catholics to the Virgin Mary. While they reverenced her as the Mother of their Lord, they found no warrant in Scripture for belief in her sinlessness. More than this they saw in the doctrine of the Immaculate Conception, and in the title given to her in much Catholic literature, "Mother of God," a tendency to break down the line of demarcation which separates Jesus Christ as God Incarnate from all other creatures, a tendency against which they feared that the distinction made by Roman Catholic theologians between different kinds of worship did not provide a sufficient safeguard.

It may be freely admitted that in the negative attitude thus taken toward the veneration of the Virgin and the saints Protestants have lost out of their religion something which Catholics find very precious.

For one thing the saints furnish the Catholic believer with examples of adventurous religion. They are his heroes and heroines, and their lives of dauntless struggle and measureless sacrifice have for young and old a perennial interest. In them the Catholic sees the virtues he admires carried to heroic heights, and the story of the obstacles that they overcame and the way they won their victory never loses its appeal.

It is not human virtues only which the Catholic admires in the saints. Their lives exhibit qualities which he has been taught to believe are characteristically divine. When he reads the life story of St. Francis of Assisi, he understands what is meant by the love of God; the stigmata make vivid to his imagination the sacrifice consummated for us on Calvary. Dearest of all and nearest is she whom every Catholic honors as the Virgin Mother of his Lord and to whom every day, and often many times each day, he addresses the prayer which is surpassed in sacredness only by the Lord's Prayer, the Ave Maria.

Henry Adams, in his book *Mont-Saint-Michel and Chartres,* a book which for a Protestant reveals an unusual insight into the genius of Catholic piety, has given an account of the role which the Virgin played in the religious life of the Middle Ages. He shows how the motherly graces attributed to her mitigated the cruelty of contemporary standards and won for her a deathless place in the affections of the faithful. Later generations have but carried the process further till Mary holds the highest place—after God—in the heavenly hierarchy.

Yet when the Protestant studies the ideal which the saint has set for himself in such standard treatises of Catholic piety, as for example, the Ascent of Mt. Carmel by St. John of the Cross, he finds something unnatural and repelling which it is difficult for him to identify with the type of simple piety of which Jesus has given us the example. *The Introduction to a Devout Life* by another Catholic saint, Francis de Sales, is more in harmony with the Protestant ideal of piety. In the familiar experiences of daily life—the life of the parent with her child, of the husband with his wife, of neighbor with neighbor—rather than in the asceticism of the solitary or the introspective piety of those who cultivate the *via negativa,* is the true genius of Protestant piety to be found.

It is not an easy ideal to which Protestants feel that God has called them but one which demands every power of heart and mind and will. Detachment is required, an inner detachment which is all the more difficult because of the lack of outward helps such as are supplied by the rules of the Catholic religious orders, or even the general rules of the Catholic Church. Selfish desires must be mastered, legitimate instincts must be sacrificed, so that the soul may dedicate itself to its primary task. Protestants, like Catholics, attain this detachment by means of contemplation and prayer. In the solitude of his room at night, or in the stillness of the early morning, the man who must act comes into touch with ultimate reality, and waits for the insight which will guide him on his way. The true test of his piety is found in what happens when he rises from his knees and goes out to meet his fellow men.

Many years ago the academic world was startled by the decision of Doctor Albert Schweitzer, the brilliant professor of theology in Strassburg, to abandon his professorship and move to Central Africa to work as a medical missionary for the victims of sleeping sickness in that desolate country. In his book, *On the Edge of the Primeval Forest,* he tells us why he went.

It was the story of Dives and Lazarus which opened Schweitzer's eyes. This parable seemed to have been spoken directly to him. In wretched Lazarus he saw the colored folk "out there in the colonies . . . who suffer from illness and pain just as much as we do, nay much more, and have absolutely no means of fighting them," while he himself was Dives, who, through his scientific knowledge of the causes of disease and pain, had "innumerable means of fighting them." And just as Dives "sinned against the poor man at his gate because for want of thought he never put himself in his place and let his heart and conscience tell him what he ought to do, so do we sin against the poor man at our gate."

The annals of foreign missions are full of such stories—the story of men like Judson or Carey or Livingstone or Paton—who turned their backs on all the world holds dear; who faced without flinching suffering of body and greater suffering of mind, yet who illustrated in signal degree the qualities of courage, decision, love, and joy, which are marks of the supernatural life.

3. The Protestant View of the Relation of Church and State

From our study of the religious life of the individual Protestant, we turn to those wider relationships in which Protestants stand to their neighbors and through which they cooperate with men of other faiths and of no faith in the economic and political life of society. We have to ask, as Father Ross has asked in his study of Catholicism, how far the political, economic and social life of a Protestant is or should be colored by his religion.

Our answer must be in principle the same as that which

Father Ross has given, that like the leaven hid in three measures of meal, religion should affect every phase of life. The acceptance, in principle, of the separation of Church and State does not mean that the Protestant feels no obligation to pass moral judgment upon the issues raised in contemporary society; only that so far as these issues are economic or political, he must deal with them in his capacity as business man, workman or citizen.

In the application of the Christian standard to the social attitude of the individual church member, the Catholic Church has on the whole been inclined to be rather more tolerant than the Protestant; thinking it more important that the individual, however imperfect, should be kept in touch with the Church, whereas Protestants, as is natural because of their history, have in theory at least, been inclined to hold church members to a higher standard than that of general society—an ideal from which it is to be feared their practice has often sadly departed.

We find here the world-old contrast between the ideal of a comprehensive and of a holy Church (what Troeltsch has called the church type and the sect type). Catholics solve this difficulty by making place in the one inclusive church for smaller bodies with stricter standards (the orders). Protestantism has, as yet, found no theoretical solution.

Individual groups have tried from time to time to commit the Church as a whole to some absolute standard, either of morals as in the case of Prohibition, of economics as in the case of Socialism, or of politics as in the case of Pacifism. But on the whole the sober sense of the Church has refused to make the identification and while it has defended the liberty of those who take the absolutist position, it has been unwilling to commit the Church as a whole to any extreme view. Among the points at which there is widespread agreement among Protestants we may include the following:

1. That the Gospel has a message for society as well as for the individual.

2. That the Church as the bearer of this message holds a unique place and responsibility among human institutions which it can surrender to no other institution, not excepting the State.

3. That man as we know him today is finite and sinful, and that sin affects every phase of his social as well as of his individual life, including his life in the Church.

4. That the fact of this imperfection does not relieve men from the responsibility of bringing Christian principles to bear upon all phases of life, not only as individuals but as members of society. Whether as parents, workers, artists, teachers or citizens, it is their duty, so far as in them lies, to act as Christians should.

5. That among human institutions the State has a position of special importance. Whether we regard it as an original creation of God or as a necessary instrument for mitigating the evil effects of sin, it has a place to fulfill in the providence of God which entitles it to the respect and, under all normal circumstances, to the obedience of the Christian.

6. That it is the responsibility of the State to maintain order in society, to protect its citizens from any attack, whether from without or from within, which threatens their security, and to secure to each of its constituent units—the family, the school, the organizations of agriculture, industry, commerce and finance—the conditions which make possible the peaceable discharge of their functions. In particular it is its duty to guarantee to the Church the

liberty which it requires for the discharge of its God-given function as witness to the Gospel.

7. That it is the duty of the Church to pay to the State the respect which is its due, to obey its laws so far as they are in accordance with the will of God as revealed in the Scripture and in history, and to inculcate upon its members the due discharge of their duties as citizens. Where, however, the State takes action which violates Christian principles, it is the responsibility of the Church to point out its fault, and where it invades the province which is the distinctive prerogative of the Church to resist at all costs.

In their interpretation of their social responsibilities there are many points in which American Protestants and American Catholics agree. A recent study made by a Committee appointed by the Federal Council of The Churches of Christ in America, shows that on most of the issues on which men divide today, the great majority of Protestants and the great majority of Catholics judge alike. If a contrast is to be made it would be not so much between the attitude of Catholics and Protestants, as between the attitude taken by the great majority of American Christians both Protestant and Catholic, and that of the American Lutherans who in their general attitude toward the State incline to a position of greater ecclesiastical aloofness. Most Lutherans would agree that when the State grants the Church freedom of worship it has under normal circumstances the right to ask political obedience; whereas most Protestants, like their Catholic fellow-Christians, believe that the Church as Church has the right and the duty to define the moral principles which should regulate the conduct of the State and where these have been violated to register its criticism.

The clearest definition of the Protestant view of the right relation between Church and State is to be found in the report of Commission II of the Oxford Conference on Life and Work. That report is as follows:

> The primary duty of the Church to the State is to be the Church, namely, to witness for God, to preach His Word, to confess the faith before men, to teach both young and old to observe the divine commandments and to serve the nation and the State by proclaiming the Will of God as the supreme standard to which all human wills must be subject and all human conduct must conform. These functions of worship, preaching, teaching and ministry the Church cannot renounce whether the State consent or not.
>
> From this responsibility certain duties follow for the Churches and for their members:
>
> (I) That of praying for the State, its people and its government;
>
> (II) That of loyalty and obedience to the State, disobedience becoming a duty only if obedience would be clearly contrary to the command of God;
>
> (III) That of cooperation with the State in promoting the welfare of the citizens, and of lending moral support to the State when it upholds the standards of justice set forth in the Word of God;
>
> (IV) That of criticism of the State when it departs from those standards;
>
> (V) That of holding before men in all their legislation and administration those principles which make for the upholding of the dignity of man who is made in the image of God;
>
> (VI) That of permeating the public life with the spirit of Christ and of training men and women who as Christians can contribute to this end.
>
> These duties rest upon Christians not only as individuals redeemed by Christ who must witness for Him in whatever position they may occupy in the State, but also upon the Church as a Christian community. The Church

can serve the State in no better way than by illustrating in its own life the kind of life which is God's Will for society as a whole. Only in the measure that it seeks to realize this mission is it in a position to rebuke the State for its sins and failures for which both individual Christians and the Church in its organized capacity have been in no small measure responsible.

In the interpretation of these duties it is important to keep in mind that as the Church in its own sphere is a universal society, so to Christian faith the individual State is not itself the ultimate political unit, but a member of a family of nations with international relations and duties which it is the responsibility not only of individual Christians but also of the Churches to affirm and to promote.

The report continues:

We recognize as essential conditions necessary to the Church's fulfillment of its primary duty that it should enjoy

(a) freedom to determine its faith and creed;

(b) freedom from any imposition by the State of religious ceremonies and forms of worship;

(c) freedom of public and private worship, preaching and teaching;

(d) freedom to determine the nature of its government and the qualifications of its ministers and members, and, conversely, the freedom of the individual to join the Church to which he feels called;

(e) freedom to control the education of its ministers, to give religious instruction to its youth, and to provide for adequate development of their religious life;

(f) freedom of Christian service and missionary activity, both home and foreign;

(g) freedom to cooperate with other Churches;

(h) freedom to use such facilities, open to all citizens or associations, as will make possible the accomplishment of these ends, as, e.g., the ownership of property and the collection of funds.

American Protestants do not deny that the liberty which they think essential for the Church may be enjoyed in countries where there is an established Church but they believe the American system of the separation of Church and State furnishes the best guarantee of that liberty. They recognize that in its practical application the principle of the separation of Church and State has had some unfortunate by-products, particularly in the field of politics, of education and of marriage and divorce. They are inclined to believe, however, that these evils, great as they are, are less than would follow from any attempt to commit to the State the enforcement of Christian principles, in matters of this kind. They are confident that the true remedy is to be found in such a progressive victory of Christian principles in the lives of the individual citizens as will make it possible to correct existing evils through their cooperation.

At one point only do we find a fundamental difference between Catholics and Protestants in their view of the relation of Church and State. Catholics and Protestants alike believe that both Church and State are divine institutions, charged with specific functions for the good of man. Both believe that under normal conditions they have a right to the obedience of the Christian. Both agree, however, that in this present transitional state they are imperfect bodies (*corpora permixta*), including in their membership and sometimes in the personnel of their government, evil men as well as good. Both agree that this being so, conditions may arise in which it will be the Christian's duty to carry his protest against a wicked State to the point of revolution. Protestants believe that the same principle applies to revolt against the Church.

4. The Place of Protestantism in the Church Universal

This concludes our brief description of the faith and life of contemporary Protestantism. It is no part of the present writer's responsibility to attempt any appraisal of the comparative value of Protestantism as a type of the religious life or to make any prophecy as to its future development. It may, however, be in place to add a few concluding comments as to the place of Protestantism in the Church Universal.

This first of all—that Protestantism is an important factor in the life of the contemporary Church. It is the form of religion through which many millions of Christians express their religious life and through which they find their relation to God deepened and purified. No plan for the future of the Christian Church can hope for success which does not make provision for the satisfaction of the type of religious need to which Protestantism owes its rise.

It is no small gain that Roman Catholics recognize this, and that in the writings of their recent spokesmen we find eloquent tribute to the vital religious experience which is to be found in the Protestant Church. Catholics do not interpret the famous phrase, *extra ecclesiam nulla salus,* as meaning that no one can be saved outside the existing Roman Catholic Church. Catholics believe that there is a soul of the Church which takes in all those who—with the light they have—are loyal to their conscience, and they believe that among those are many loyal Protestants with whom they hope to have still closer fellowship in the life to come. Protestants on their part no longer believe that the Pope "is antichrist, that man of sin, and son of perdition, that exalteth himself in the Church against Christ and all that is called God."[1] They recognize that in the Catholic Church there is a stream of piety at which they are happy to drink and include among their choicest treasures the lives of the great saints who have found their inspiration in the Church of Rome.

There is a wide field then, in which Catholics and Protestants can cooperate with mutual self-respect—the field of scholarship, of social service, of benevolence and mercy. There are great moral and political issues in which they will be found in the future, as in the past, standing side by side. Catholics will no doubt continue to see in Catholicism the purest and final form of religion, and will hope and believe that in due time Protestants will come to recognize this and find their way into the Catholic fold. Protestants will continue to believe that God has laid upon them the responsibility of witnessing to essential aspects of Christian life and truth; aspects for which Catholics as well as mankind in general are their debtors. They dare to hope that in the Church Universal of which they feel themselves a part, Protestants will have a place with Catholics in the all-embracing family of God.

But if this place is to be worthily filled and this witness effectively borne, Protestants will need to take far more seriously than they have yet done, their responsibility for achieving inner Protestant unity. This need not necessarily mean (at least not in the immediate present) organic unity in the sense of bringing into existence a single all-embracing institution. It may take the form of some kind of federal union such as we see in the United States or of which the Eastern Orthodox Churches furnish an example; but it must do two things which Protestantism in

1 Original quotation from Westminster Confession of Faith, since revised.

its present form is not able to do today. It must create a consciousness of spiritual unity which makes all who call themselves Protestant aware that they belong to a single Church, and it must create the agency through which that consciousness of spiritual unity can find united expression.

One reason why Protestants have been so slow in dealing with the second part of this responsibility is that they have already gone a long way toward achieving the first. Over wide areas Protestants of different denominations feel their membership in the one Church and recognize their fellow Protestants of other names as fellow Churchmen. The outward mark of this inward unity is the widespread practice of intercommunion.

But spiritual unity alone is not enough. Christians must be able to act as well as to think and to feel together. Here the present condition of the Protestant Churches presents all but insuperable obstacles. Here and there a beginning has been made through various federal agencies, national and local, but they touch only a small part of the life of the Church, and over wide areas the competitive principle still holds sway. Here the Catholic Church through its diocesan system sets an example of order which Protestantism will do well to emulate. In the modern world where science is tying the nations more and more closely together, the principle of unrestricted sovereignty may work havoc both for Church and for State. Catholicism solves this problem in one way: by concentrating all authority in a single institution. Protestantism, to justify its own claim that it is possible to achieve unity through freedom, must show that another way is possible.

Here the Ecumenical Movement is pointing the way. It is pointing the way in theory by its generous recognition of the truth and goodness in different forms of Christian life. It is pointing the way in practice by furnishing in the plan for a World Council of Churches the framework of an organization through which Christians can express their unity in the things in which they agree while they carry on common study of the things in which they differ. It is showing that it is possible even now for Christians of the Catholic and Protestant types to work, to study and to worship together. While their principles, as Father Ross has explained them, do not make it possible for Catholics of the Roman type to take a formal part in the Ecumenical Movement, at least they can welcome it as a step toward a wider unity and pray for the success of those who have its good at heart.

In the meantime we may rejoice in every indication of better understanding and mutual respect which the times make possible and hope that they may increase in the years to come. It is the writer's hope, as he is sure it is that of Father Ross and Rabbi Finkelstein, that this symposium may prove a modest contribution to this increased understanding and respect.

APPENDIX

Affirmation of Union in Allegiance to Our Lord Jesus Christ *

We are one in faith in our Lord Jesus Christ, the incarnate Word of God. We are one in allegiance to Him as Head of the church, and as King of Kings and Lord of Lords. We are one in acknowledging that this allegiance takes precedence of any other allegiance that may make claims upon us.

This unity does not consist in the agreement of our minds or the consent of our wills. It is founded in Jesus Christ Himself, who lived, died, and rose again to bring us to the Father, and who through the Holy Spirit dwells in His church. We are one because we are all the objects of the love and grace of God, and called by Him to witness in all the world to His glorious gospel.

Our unity is of heart and spirit. We are divided in the outward forms of our life in Christ, because we understand differently His will for His church. We believe, however, that a deeper understanding will lead us towards a united apprehension of the truth as it is in Jesus.

We humbly acknowledge that our divisions are contrary to the will of Christ, and we pray God in His mercy to shorten the days of our separation and to guide us by His Spirit into fullness of unity.

* Adopted by the Second World Conference on Faith and Order, held in Edinburgh in August, 1937.

We are thankful that during recent years we have been drawn together; prejudices have been overcome, misunderstandings removed, and real, if limited, progress has been made towards our goal of a common mind.

In this conference we may gratefully claim that the Spirit of God has made us willing to learn from one another, and has given us a fuller vision of the truth and enriched our spiritual experience.

We have lifted up our hearts together in prayer; we have sung the same hymns; together we have read the same Holy Scriptures. We recognise in one another, across the barriers of our separation, a common Christian outlook and a common standard of values. We are therefore assured of a unity deeper than our divisions.

We are convinced that our unity of spirit and aim must be embodied in a way that will make it manifest to the world, though we do not yet clearly see what outward form it should take.

We believe that every sincere attempt to cooperate in the concerns of the kingdom of God draws the severed communions together in increased mutual understanding and good will. We call upon our fellow Christians of all communions to practice such cooperation; to consider patiently occasions of disunion that they may be overcome; to be ready to learn from those who differ from them; to seek to remove those obstacles to the furtherance of the gospel in the non-Christian world which arise from our divisions; and constantly to pray for that unity which we believe to be our Lord's will for His church.

We desire also to declare to all men everywhere our assurance that Christ is the one hope of unity for the world in face of the distractions and dissensions of this present time. We know that our witness is weakened by our divisions. Yet we are one in Christ and in the fellowship of His Spirit. We pray that everywhere, in a world divided and perplexed, men may turn to Jesus Christ our Lord, who makes us one in spite of our divisions; that He may bind in one those who by many worldly claims are set at variance; and that the world may at last find peace and unity in Him; to whom be glory for ever.

INDEX

INDEX

INDEX

INDEX